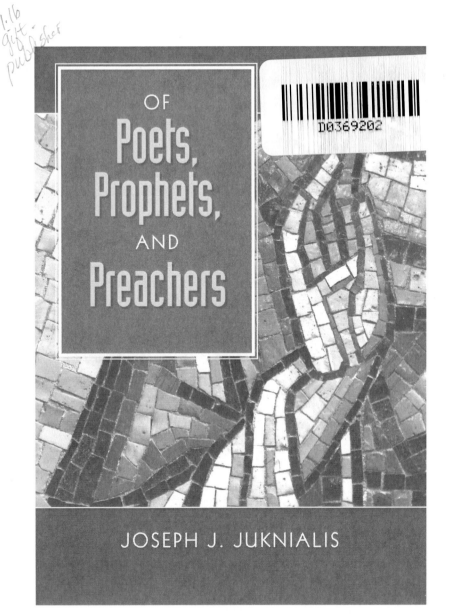

OF
Poets,
Prophets,
AND
Preachers

JOSEPH J. JUKNIALIS

[[]LP] [P]
World Library Publications
the music and liturgy division of J.S.Paluch Company, Inc.

3708 River Road, Suite 400
Franklin Park, IL 60131-2158
800-566-6150 • wlpcs@jspaluch.com • wlpmusic.com

Author: Joseph J. Juknialis
Editor: Michael E. Novak
Copy Editor: Marcia T. Lucey
Cover Design: Christine Broquet
Book Design: Denise Durand Walsh
Director of Publications: Mary Beth Kunde-Anderson
Production Manager: Deb Johnston

WLP 017114
ISBN 978-1-58459-803-9

Contents

Introduction 5

1. Rooted in the Scriptures 9

2. Brings Forth Wonder and Awe 17

3. Descriptive, Not Prescriptive 23

4. Challenging 29

5. Only One Message 37

6. Appeals to Our Hearts 43

7. Appeals to Our Minds 51

8. Tells the Story of the Community 59

9. Presumes That Those Gathered Are Good People 69

10. Leaves the Assembly with Hope 75

A Summary of the Questions 82

Introduction

As we grow into adulthood and independence, we all come to realize quickly that if we want to eat and not go hungry, we have three options. We can go to restaurants; we can find someone to cook for us; we can learn how to cook. A daily diet of restaurant fare can become either quite demanding on a budget or unhealthy and rather boring from the fast-food window. Without someone at hand to do my cooking for me, I realized early on that I needed to learn how to cook. So I have not gone hungry, even if I have not become a gourmet cook by any stretch of the definition. Still, I have learned how to use a slow cooker, boil pasta and toss in some meatballs and sauce, and put together a meatloaf. If I want to take the time, or on a special occasion, I can follow a recipe and do something a bit more complicated, but not by much. In the process I have come to realize that recipes do two things. One, they list the ingredients; and two, they give instructions about how to put those ingredients together. Some recipes will also include a picture of the completed dish. I find it quite helpful to know what the meal should look like.

This book is about the ingredients that go into effective liturgical preaching. It will not tell you how to put those ingredients together. That is a task for another book or another author. However, as with preparing a meal, it is helpful to know what goes into the process. As an aid to knowing what the finished product should look like, the following list describes what a person who listens to a homily might hope to hear, rather like the picture of the completed dish that appears with a recipe.

1. A homily is **ROOTED IN THE SCRIPTURES** that are proclaimed at that particular liturgical gathering. Though a homily is not a Bible-study explanation of those texts, the liturgical homily does tell how God continues to act in our own lives just as God did long ago. *Listen for how God's story and your story are the same story.*

2. A homily **BRINGS FORTH WONDER AND AWE.** Believers trust that God is ever present, all around us. Yet that presence is not always obvious. Often God seems hidden, and God's presence needs to be pointed out. *Be open to the surprise of God's presence where you had not expected to find it.*

3. A homily is **DESCRIPTIVE, NOT PRESCRIPTIVE.** Actions speak louder than words, so we are moved more by a story describing someone's goodness than by a command that we be good. Like nagging, telling people what to do does not change behavior. *Listen for stories that describe how God has been experienced and how others have responded to that experience.*

4. A homily is **CHALLENGING** and thought-provoking without instilling guilt. When we hear the life stories of those who have faithfully lived out the gospel, God's Spirit moves our own hearts to want to live in that same way. It is not the preacher's task to move hearts. That's the task of the Spirit. *Listen for where you are being stretched.*

5. A homily has **ONLY ONE MESSAGE.** Not four, not two, just one. An effective homily is between seven and ten minutes in length, so there's not much time to say more than one thing and say it well. *Attend to that one message.*

6. A homily **APPEALS TO OUR HEARTS**. It touches our emotions, in some ways like a poem or a piece of music or a walk through nature, moving us to appreciate the wonders of our God. If after a homily you feel like singing or dancing or applauding with your heart, then your spirit has been touched. *Listen for the homiletic image that speaks to you.*

7. A homily also **APPEALS TO OUR MINDS**. While it may not be a theological explanation of some doctrine or truth, a homily does have something to say to our understanding of life. *Listen for some wisdom.*

8. A homily **TELLS THE STORY OF THE COMMUNITY**. Scripture is primarily for the community. Only in a secondary fashion is it for individuals and personal spirituality. Consequently, a homily points to how God is working by means of the rhythms of culture, in the Church, in society, in the parish and neighborhood. *Listen for the story of the entire community.*

9. The preacher **PRESUMES THAT THOSE GATHERED ARE GOOD PEOPLE** who seek to live their faith according to the gospel. *Listen for the story of your goodness*, of how God works in your life and of how you are already living God's word.

10. A homily **LEAVES THE ASSEMBLY WITH HOPE**. Believers should leave with the recognition that their God is with them, leading and guiding and sustaining. They should not depart from the eucharistic gathering depressed or guilt-ridden or oppressed with heavy burdens. Our God provides us a future. Hope is believing both that such a future is already happening and that it will be fully realized. *Listen for the promise of that future.*

Each of the chapters in this book reflects upon one of these ingredients or aspects of an effective homily. In that sense this book is primarily for those who preach. However, those who listen to homilies may also find this book helpful to enrich their listening to the homilies that they hear in their parishes. For those who preach, admittedly it can be difficult to preach in a way that always includes all ten aspects in every homily. That is the ideal, however, and over the course of a year all ten of these aspects can make their way into our preaching.

Preaching out of the scriptures, preaching only one message, preaching that presumes those who have gathered are good people—such qualities seem to come more easily perhaps because those qualities can be more intentional. Such qualities should be present in every homily. To be creative with an image, however, or to have some new insight to offer, or to preach in a way that elicits wonder and awe—such preaching seems to be more dependent upon the movement of God's Spirit. Creativity and imagination do not always show up on demand. As to the effectiveness of our preaching, none of us really knows. We need to ask those who sit in the pews.

In all of this there is an element of the **Poet**—that aspect of creativity and imagination that captures both hearts and spirits. The objection that one is not creative is simply not valid. Pastors find ways of trimming budgets, working through the conflicts of staff disagreements, motivating parishioners to volunteer, and forming new ministries. All of that takes creativity and imagination. There is much research that shows that if one is able to be creative in one area, one is also able to be creative in another.

Preaching is also called to show the face of the **Prophet**. As always the challenge is to speak the truth in such a way that it is not compromised, but in such a way that it is heard with open ears so that justice is embraced.

In the final analysis it is the **Preacher** who is called to be the spiritual director of the faith community. The task is always to point to God's activity in the lives of those present in the assembly, to nurture the weak, to encourage when there is fear, and to affirm those who live in faith-filled discipleship.

To some these roles of Poet and Prophet and Preacher may seem daunting, and well they could be if we who preach don't trust that God's Spirit will do its work when we are faithful to our calling. It was Jesus who long ago came as Poet and Prophet and Preacher. We who are his ministers can seek to do no less.

CHAPTER I

Rooted
in the Scriptures

Families tell stories to remember who they are. Those who grow up without a family, without stories to tell, will often have a sense of undiscovered identity, a kind of hole in the picture of their life.

All four of my grandparents came to this country from Lithuania. They came when they were single, settled in Sheboygan, Wisconsin, married, and as it turned out ended up living next door to one another. All of that was before they ever became my grandparents and some time before the daughter of one family and the son of the other fell in love and eventually became my mother and father.

In the first years of my life I spoke only Lithuanian simply because it was the language of that small extended family. English came when I began to explore my back yard and the back yards of the neighborhood kids on the block. Shortly after my brother John was born, four years my junior, we moved to Fond du Lac. John was never immersed in the same Lithuanian culture, much to the dismay of my grandfather. And so once John made his way into grade school my grandfather told him he would pay John ten cents for every Lithuanian word he would memorize up to a hundred words. Eager to make some quick cash, John readily agreed, made some money, and was tested and paid each year for years to come. The offer was never made to me. I simply already knew the vocabulary from growing up with it. To this day John can remember scattered words, though I have quite forgotten what I knew. Differing functions of different parts of the human brain, I suspect.

I share that story because it is a part of what it means to be our family. Again and again, at least once a year, John will find an opportunity to tell the story and then begin to recite what words he can remember, even though many have faded with time. Yet telling the story is a part of how both he and I know who we are. So it is with most families and the stories they tell.

Elie Wiesel is a Holocaust survivor, author, and activist. He tells the story of the Holocaust lest the horror of those years be forgotten. He recounts numerous Hasidic parables and tales of Jewish life and history so the Jewish people will remember who they are. One such story is recounted in the prologue to his novel *The Gates of the Forest*.

> When the great Rabbi Israel Baal Shem-Tov saw misfortune threatening the Jews it was his custom to go into a certain part of the forest to meditate. There he would light a fire, say a special prayer, and the miracle would be accomplished and the misfortune averted.

> Later, when his disciple, the celebrated Magid of Mezritch, had occasion, for the same reason, to intercede with heaven, he would go to the same place in the forest and say: "Master of the Universe, listen! I do not know how to light the fire, but I am still able to say the prayer," and again the miracle would be accomplished.

> Still later, Rabbi Moshe-Leib of Sasov, in order to save his people once more, would go into the forest and say: "I do not know how to light the fire, I do not know the prayer, I know the place and this must be sufficient." It was sufficient and the miracle was accomplished.

Then it fell to Rabbi Israel of Rizhyn to overcome misfortune. Sitting in his armchair, his head in his hands, he spoke to God: "I am unable to light the fire and I do not know the prayer; I cannot even find the place in the forest. All I can do is to tell the story, and this must be sufficient." And it was sufficient.

God made man because he loves stories.[1]

When God Speaks

Families, communities, and nations all tell their stories in order to remember who they are. That is why people of faith tell the stories of their God, so that they too remember who they are. Year after year we tell the biblical stories of God's events in our lives. We do so lest we forget, and so we remember. It is why in the Christian religion, in all of our traditions, we preach from the sacred scriptures. Having listened to how God once moved and acted in the lives of the Hebrew people and in the person of Jesus, we then listen in the homily to how God continues to move and act in our own lives, even in our own day in the very same way. That is what a homily does. *It points to where God is doing today what God did then.*

What God did then was to speak. There are many aspects common to God's modes of communication and our own. For both God and us humans the words we use reveal who we are; they call us into relationships; they shape our reality because they can bring about the experience of love or peace or hurt or fear. The one difference is that for the most part when we speak we almost always use verbal language, words that others can hear. The words of God, on the other hand, are usually events. Thus the sacred scriptures, to which we often refer as the word of God, are really like cousins once removed

---

[1] Excerpt from *Gates of the Forest* by Elie Wiesel, translation copyright © 1966 and renewed 1994 by Henry Holt and Company, Inc. Used by permission of Schocken Books, an imprint of the Knopf Doubleday Publishing Group, a division of Penguin Random House LLC. All rights reserved. Any third party use of this material, outside of this publication, is prohibited. Interested parties must apply to Penguin Random House LLC for permission.

from that word. The true word of God is the event of God's interaction with the people of God. It was the Exodus event, the Exile, the times they saw themselves being punished by their God and redeemed by their God, and ultimately the event of the Lord Jesus. The written book we call the Bible is in reality a community's interpretation of those events over time, the events that God once spoke. Those events are the actual word of God, and for us who say we are believers they are normative; that is to say, they are the pattern by which we understand our own lives. In every age God still speaks those same words. God continues to speak if only we have ears to hear, which in reality is to say if only we have eyes to see.

The Salvific, Prophetic, and Creative Word

The word of God continues to be **salvific**, revealing that we are saved from darkness and death. Many years ago I found myself sitting in a pew at a communal reconciliation service and listening to a homily about the mercy of God. The Gospel was the story of the woman caught in adultery. For the most part the homily was what any of us would expect. God loves us, God offers mercy, God heals. But then the homilist made a statement that has stayed with me for the next forty years of my life—that God does not make it difficult to experience forgiveness. In fact God makes it easy, lest we stay away from Love, from the life our God offers. The statement by the homilist that day was certainly not anything revolutionary, but it was apparently what I needed to hear at that moment in my life. It has stayed with me ever since. In my mind's eye I can still see the preacher, the pew in which I was sitting, the setting of that parish church. That word of God proclaimed has been **salvific** for me ever since.

The word of God is also **prophetic.** It proclaims a vision different from the one that we happen to be living, and it challenges us to live by that new vision. After my first parish assignment as a priest I was reassigned to a new parish. I liked the people in that new parish. I felt I was making some small difference. I was happy. After four years the placement board of the archdiocese called and asked if I would be willing to move to another parish. A move seemed too early for my own rhythms, and in addition that proposed parish had difficulties.

It had a reputation for being quite traditional, something I knew would not make it easy for me. And the pastor had a history of difficulties with associate pastors. And I was just beginning to settle in and be comfortable where I was. I considered the request and decided against the move. The board, however, asked if I wouldn't take a bit more time to reconsider. What harm would that be, I thought, so I agreed and again decided against the change of assignment. A week later they called once more with the same request that I reconsider.

That weekend was the feast of the Body and Blood of Christ. The Gospel was that of the multiplication of the loaves and fishes, in which Jesus took bread, blessed it, broke it, and gave it to the people to eat. The message I had decided to preach that weekend was that we become the Body of Christ whenever we take our lives, bless them, and then break them open to be given to others. I suddenly became aware of the contradiction I would live if I preached that message but was not willing to live it myself by going where I did not want to go, by going where it seemed God could be calling me. It was a message for my own life that I did not want to hear. In the end that **prophetic** word compelled me to say yes to the placement board.

Finally, the word of God is **creative.** Listening to it Sunday after Sunday slowly reshapes our worldview into one that takes on the hues and tones of God's worldview. We drive by a stranded motorist and find ourselves thinking of the story of the Good Samaritan. We may stop or we may drive on by but the image of caring for the abandoned one echoes in us. We might be someone who suffers and struggles with life, and so we find ourselves thinking of Jesus' agony in the Garden of Gethsemane. In the midst of grief and death we find ourselves turning to the image of the Good Shepherd who brings the lost home. The stories of scripture have created a new world for us in which to live because God is continuing to create a new heaven and a new earth.

God's Stories, Our Stories

The point that I am seeking to make is that the stories of God who acts ceaselessly amid the people are also our stories. Adam and Eve were expelled from the Garden of Eden and we begin to realize that we too have been excluded from the best of life. We may have been alienated by a son or daughter and find ourselves unable to keep contact with our grandchildren. We may have had a serious illness all our life and feel that somehow we have been treated unfairly, excluded from many of the marvelous things that others enjoy doing. It may be that we have never found love, someone with whom to share our life, and so we feel that we have been denied. The story of Adam and Eve who longed for God's goodness is our story.

Joseph, the son of Jacob, was sold into slavery by his brothers, his own kin. We may feel we have been sold out by those we love, perhaps forced into a divorce we did not choose, or finding ourselves in a family divided over an inheritance. The story of Joseph can be our story, yet also a story that ends with God bringing about healing.

The story of Moses standing at the burning bush may bring to us poignant memories of God's presence in our own life—moments made holy at the birth of a child or being confronted by great beauty or the wonder of falling in love. The story of Moses discovering God's call and presence is surely our story as well.

Jesus cried over the city of Jerusalem for what its citizens failed to recognize, and he cried at the death of Lazarus. Surely we have cried over those loved ones who seem to have lost their way and over those who have died. The story of Jesus' tears is our story, too.

The story of Zacchaeus, who wanted to see Jesus and climbed a sycamore tree to do so, seems to tell our story of seeking holiness and the presence of God in our lives, and when found, how that presence moves us to live differently. The story of Zaccheus is certainly our story.

Such liturgical preaching, that names the stories of God in human life, was called for in the Second Vatican Council's *Constitution on the Sacred Liturgy*, 35: "The sermon, moreover, should draw its content mainly from scriptural and liturgical sources, for it is the proclamation of God's wonderful works in the history of salvation, which is the mystery of Christ ever made present and active in us, especially in the celebration of the liturgy."[2] Thus the task of the preacher is not only to remind us of how God once spoke with mighty deeds to shape a people. It is more than that. The task of the preacher is to point out where those mighty deeds continue to take place in our own day. As noted in the recently published *Homiletic Directory*, "Discerning again and again the pattern of Christ's death and resurrection in the life of the community and the world . . . will strongly shape the content of the homily."[3] When people begin to recognize that pattern, then faith happens and faith deepens. Such is the terrible task that is entrusted to those who are called to preach, to nourish the faith journey of those who sit before them by rooting the vision of their own lives in the sacred scriptures.

 **The Preacher asks, "Where do I find the biblical stories of this Sunday echoed in the personal and communal events of this past week?"**

---

[2] Second Vatican Council, *Sacrosanctum concilium* (Constitution on the Sacred Liturgy), December 4, 1963, art. 35.

[3] Vatican Congregation for Divine Worship and the Discipline of the Sacraments, *Homiletic Directory*. Vatican City: *Libreria Editrice Vaticana*, 2015, par. 33.

CHAPTER 2

Brings Forth Wonder and Awe

There are flashes of transcendence in our lives, instances when we see the world in a different light, and we think maybe we have been touched by God. Such sudden seeing doesn't often happen, but when it does we remember it. We do not forget the moment.

Many years ago, when I was in my late twenties and on a retreat, I found myself early one morning walking through a field of wild daisies. Each was no bigger than a dime. In the darkness of the nighttime, cobwebs had been draped upon them like lace doilies, and the morning's dew glistened in the sun. It seemed idyllic, and I simply stood there immersed in it all. At that moment I wasn't thinking about anything in particular and certainly not praying, at least not intentionally the way that we are usually encouraged to do. It was probably more a daydream than anything else. Then for a moment, just a moment and no more, I came to realize somehow that what was at the heart of being a wild daisy and what was at the heart of me being me were exactly the same thing. And that same thing, I thought to myself at the time and still do, was the presence of God. And if it was true of me and wild daisies, then it seemed to me that it must be true of all creation. Somehow all of creation is one because at the heart of all creation is a divine presence, like a river that flows through everything touching everything, as a young high school girl once described God to me. I have never forgotten that moment in a field on retreat in central Wisconsin. None of us do forget if we should come upon a time such as that. Suddenly we see the world lit differently.

That too is what good preaching does to us, and that is what most of us want it to do. We would like someone to open our heart just because we know down deep we cannot do it for ourselves. And if someone can do that for us, we think, then maybe it just might be possible that we could live more faithfully. That is what we hope for when the Gospel proclamation ends, and we sit down in the pew and open ourselves to the preacher who stands there before us.

Seeing God in Relationship

In his letter to Timothy, Saint Paul notes that "[a]ll scripture is inspired by God and is useful for teaching, for refutation, for correction, and for training in righteousness" (2 Timothy 3:16). Over the centuries preaching has taken on one or another of these purposes, shifting back and forth depending upon the needs of the age. The Fathers used the pulpit to teach the truths of faith with images akin to poetry. During the time of the Reformation Catholic preaching took on the air of refutation and apologetics as it sought to defend itself against the reformers. In the early half of the twentieth century preaching became catechetical, both teaching doctrine and seeking to encourage moral living and so avoid sin. Since the Second Vatican Council liturgical preaching has been focused upon righteousness, which is to say that the world and God are in relationship. The focus of our preaching is seeing the world lit through and through with the presence of God. In other words, it is the *kerygma* that we proclaim when we preach, the death and resurrection of the Lord Jesus as it continues to be made manifest in our lives today. As noted in the document *Preaching the Mystery of Faith*, "Every homily . . .

must therefore be about the dying and rising of Jesus Christ and his sacrificial passage through suffering to new and eternal life for us."[4] It is discovering and realizing the wonderful acts of God taking place in our personal lives as well as in the rhythms of our communities and in all of creation that bring us to wonder and awe.

Yet seeing with the eyes of faith when we are blind in so many ways is not done easily. It takes time to see differently a world that is lit with God's presence. We think we see, while in reality we are often blind and don't know that we need to see. Emilie Griffin describes what it is like when someone who has been born blind is enabled to see for the first time because of modern medicine.

> The patient on opening his eyes gets little or no enjoyment; indeed, he finds the experience painful. He reports only a spinning mass of light and colors. He proves to be quite unable to pick up objects by sight, to recognize what they are, or to name them. He has no conception of space with objects in it, although he knows all about objects and their names by touch. "Of course," you will say, "he must take a little time to learn to recognize them by sight." Not a little time, but a very long time, in fact, years. His brain has not been trained in the rules of seeing. We are not conscious that there are any such rules; we think we see, as we say, naturally. But we have in fact learned a whole set of rules during childhood.[5]

Modern men and women live in a world that swirls with sights, sounds, and stimuli that are designed to appeal to all five senses. Recognizing the hand of God in the midst of it all can be difficult, in part because much of it can be the hand of God disguised. It can be challenging to name what is the work of God and what is not. How to see rightly, then, becomes the question as well as the task of the preacher. So Sunday after Sunday the preacher brings to those in the assembly a new

---

[4] United States Conference of Catholic Bishops (USCCB), *Preaching the Mystery of Faith: The Sunday Homily*, 15.

[5] Emilie Griffin, *Souls in Full Sail*, 143-144. Copyright © 2011 by Emilie Griffin. Used by permission of InterVarsity Press, P.O. Box 1400, Downers Grove, IL 60515 USA. www.ivpress.com.

way of seeing. Because seeing rightly does not happen all at once, because in fact it takes a lifetime, the preacher names for those in the pews the concrete ways God is moving in their lives. Little by little, Sunday by Sunday, together they grow, preacher and faithful, recognizing that they have not been abandoned by their God, but on the contrary are being refashioned into the image of the Lord Jesus in good times and bad, in sickness and in health, in joys and in sorrows, in the midst of their sin and in their grace.

Yet for us to see God playing in our world, shaping our lives and our loves, delighting to be our God as well as being the One who redirects and reforms and recreates—well, that just seems to be too much for us to recognize.

William Irwin Thompson describes the difficulty this way: "We are like flies crawling across the ceiling of the Sistine Chapel. We cannot see what angels and gods lie underneath the threshold of our perceptions. We do not live in reality; we live in our paradigms, our habituated perceptions, our illusions we share through culture we call reality, but the true reality of our condition is invisible."[6]

The liturgical preacher, then, must be a person of faith, one who sees what others long to see but do not. He or she must be so immersed in the ongoing presence of the Incarnation in everyday living that he or she continually seeks out the river that flows through everything, struggling to name it and give it voice. In that process the preacher becomes filled with the mystery of wonder and awe.

Preaching by Mystery

One of the truths of the Catholic tradition is that good theology and good science cannot contradict each other. Yet at the same time, because our time in history is so colored by science, many find themselves unable to live with mystery. In their minds, if it cannot be explained it must not be true or must not exist. On the other hand, to believe in the Incarnation is to live in mystery and to be awed by it.

---

[6] William Irwin Thompson, *Evil and World Order* (New York: Harper & Row, 1976), 81. Copyright © 1976 by William Irwin Thompson. Reprinted courtesy of HarperCollins Publishers.

Kathleen Dean Moore is chair of the Department of Philosophy at Oregon State University, where she works to make connections among ideas and nature and the written word. She writes of a time she took a group of college students on a retreat into the wilderness of the Northwest. A young student named Carrie told a story as they gathered around a campfire:

"This is a story my father gave me. His grandfather gave it to him. I am giving it to you." Carrie spoke from the darkness beyond the fire's circle of light. "A long time ago, the people were asleep in their village when they heard a great crashing in the forest. The warriors leapt to their feet and children hid in their robes. Everyone was frightened by the sound of a strong wind, the cracking of branches, thunderous thumping. In the morning, the men of the village went out to see what had happened. They found a long trail of broken branches and upended soil. All the cottonwoods had left the forest and marched to the edge of the river. That's where the men found the trees in the morning. And no one knows why."

The students stirred in their lawn chairs. The fire popped and a stream of sparks rose past the pines.

"So," Carrie said, "what's the most important part of this story?

I didn't know. No one knew. I was afraid to guess . . .

The most important part is the last sentence; that no one knows why the trees went to the river. It's a mystery." Carrie paused.

"Is mystery a good thing, or a bad thing?"

Silence still.

"I believe mystery *is* a good thing. The great mystery isn't an enemy to fight or a hole to fill. It's a source of strength and comfort. The existence of so much that we don't understand is a gift to us. That great mystery is what wildness is, and wildness is a great mystery."[7]

---

[7] Kathleen Dean Moore, *The Pine Island Paradox: Making Connections in a Disconnected World*, 98–99. Copyright © 2004 by Kathleen Dean Moore. Reprinted with permission of Milkweed Editions, Minneapolis, MN. www.milkweed.org

Mystery *is* a good thing. When we surrender to it, when we embrace it, then it reveals to us the presence of God in our lives.

So then how does one preach without destroying mystery? How does one preach in a way that makes it possible for the believers who listen to be moved to wonder and awe? No one can guarantee such a response simply because that is the work of the Spirit. Nevertheless, when the preacher presumes to give answers, when the preacher attempts to explain all of the aspects of life that confound us, then he or she strips our lives of all mystery. On the other hand, the preacher can prepare the path for the Spirit to do its work by pointing concretely to how and where God is moving in everyday life, by telling the stories of God in life. As the preacher does so, the hearers begin to recognize their own lives in the telling. When that realization happens, then they find themselves lost in the wonder of how their lives are filled with God. Indeed, our lives are the story of God. Most often when that occurs they are not moments of ecstasy or spiraling dizziness. Most often they are the moments when any of us simply and quietly sit back and smile to ourselves over the fact that we are so blessed with the movement of God in our own comings and goings. And then we quietly say to ourselves, "Amen."

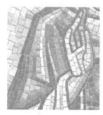 **The Poet asks, "Where or how did God's presence surprise me in ways I had not expected or seen before?"**

CHAPTER 3

Descriptive, Not Prescriptive

We were talking of dragons, Tolkien and I
In a Berkshire bar. The big workman
Who had sat silent and sucked his pipe
All evening, from his empty mug
With gleaming eye, glanced toward us:
"I seen 'em myself!" he said fiercely.[8]

—C.S. Lewis

Many years ago I attended a workshop on pastoral counseling. The presenter was himself a priest with a background in psychology. I still recall an observation he made from his own experience. He told us that it took him twenty years of priestly ministry to realize that when someone said to him, "Father, could I talk to you?" what they were asking was just that—to talk to him. They were not interested in *him*

---

[8] C.S. Lewis, "The Alliterative Metre," in *Selected Literary Essays*, ed. Walter Hooper (London: Cambridge University Press, 1969), 18.

talking to *them*. They were interested in having someone listen to their story. It is a rare gift for someone to sit and listen to us fully and attentively. When someone does, we have a sense that we have been understood and valued.

When we hear someone tell a story that echoes our own experience, that too creates a sense of being understood. That simple truth is echoed in the quote from C.S. Lewis at the beginning of this chapter. My own theory, or perhaps suspicion, is that the movies we remember, the ones that we really enjoy and are interested in seeing more than once, and the television programs that are our favorites—they are the ones that tell our own stories, or perhaps at least the ones we wish were our stories. My own favorite film has long been *Dead Poets Society*. In the film Robin Williams plays John Keating, a teacher of English literature in a boys' boarding school. He is able to spark an interest in and even love for poetry in the minds and hearts of his students. They find themselves captivated by the images that poetry elicits. At one of their gatherings in the dark of night the students read Henry David Thoreau to one another by flashlight. "I went to the woods because I wished to live deliberately, to front only the essential facts of life, and see if I could not learn what it had to teach, and not, when I came to die, discover that I had not lived. . . . I wanted to live deep and suck out all the marrow of life, to live so sturdily and Spartan-like as to put to rout all that was not life."[9] I suppose the film is a favorite of mine because besides enjoying poetry, I have spent a lifetime preaching that sort of message, that there is more to life than what we live on the surface. That what is real is invisible and what is visible is only a shadow of what is real. Is that not what faith is all about? That is why I preach. I think that is why I like that film. It tells my story. Is that not why you like the films and stories you do, because they tell your own story? We feel understood then and perhaps validated for who we are.

So then the task of the preacher is to tell the stories of God acting in our lives and in our world, and to tell those stories in such a way that listeners begin to realize that the preacher is describing their very lives. We do not hunger for someone to

---

[9] Henry David Thoreau, *Walden*, paragraph 16.

tell us what to do, to prescribe a set of behaviors for our lives. We do hunger for someone to understand us and so describe our lives and how it is with us. This is because often we do not realize how God is present in what we are all about, and we need someone to show us.

Finding God's Story

Such stories of God's activity are found in countless places. Surely they occur in our own lives, and those are the ones we treasure most, but they also arise in films and television, in sports and music, in novels and poetry and drama, in the rhythms of society and the rhythms of our own psyches, in the politics of government and the events of nations. Nothing is exempt. Why? Because of the Incarnation, God has become enfleshed in all of life. And because of the resurrection of the Lord Jesus, Christ has been set free. So what we do as preachers is proclaim this Resurrection. It is the *kerygma*, the ongoing dying and rising of the Lord Jesus throughout all of time. Those are the stories we tell as preachers, the ones that describe the *kerygma* taking place. It is all in process. It is what the Jesuit priest and French philosopher and paleontologist Father Pierre Teilhard de Chardin was referring to when he wrote: "Above all, trust in the slow work of God. We are quite naturally impatient in everything to reach the end without delay. We should like to skip the intermediate stages. We are impatient of being on the way to something unknown, something new. And yet it is the law of all progress that it is made by passing through some stages of instability—and that it may take a very long time."[10] It is those intermediate stages of God's work that we describe when we preach.

In the documents of the Second Vatican Council the Church itself has encouraged us to make use of all such sources in communicating the gospel.

> Theologians are now being asked, within the
> methods and limits of the science of theology, to
> seek out more efficient ways—provided the meaning
> and understanding of them is safeguarded—of

---

[10] Teilhard de Chardin, quoted in Michael Harter, *Hearts on Fire* (St. Louis: Institute of Jesuit Sources, 1993), 58. Used by permission.

presenting their teaching to modern man: for the deposit and truths of the faith are one thing, the manner of expressing them is quite another. In pastoral care sufficient use should be made, not only of theological principles, but also of the findings of secular sciences, especially psychology and sociology: in this way the faithful will be brought to a purer and more mature living of the faith.

In their own way literature and art are very important in the life of the Church. They seek to give expression to man's nature, his problems, and his experience in an effort to discover and perfect man himself and the world in which he lives; they try to discover his place in history and in the universe, to throw light on his suffering and his joy, his needs and his potentialities, and to outline a happier destiny in store for him. Hence they can elevate human life, which they express under many forms according to various times and places.

. . . Thus the knowledge of God will be made better known; the preaching of the Gospel will be rendered more intelligible to man's mind and will appear more relevant to his situation.[11]

Preaching in a way that describes the activity of God in the lives and hearts of all the various individuals who sit in the pews on any Sunday morning is no small task. How to do so, in short, is the power of story. How is it that oldsters and youngsters, teens and their parents, the wise and the simple can all watch the same movie or television program and be captivated by it? It is how stories communicate. Each person sees the story through the lens of his or her own life. Each person is drawn into it by their own history and their own world view. Barbara Hardy has observed that narrative "is a primary act of mind transferred to art from life itself . . . For we dream in narrative, daydream in narrative, remember, anticipate, hope, despair, believe, doubt, plan, revise, criticize,

---

[11] Second Vatican Council, *Gaudium et spes* (The Church in the Modern World), December 7, 1965, art. 62.

construct, gossip, learn, hate, and love by narrative."[12] It is true, we live in terms of narratives, and thus it makes sense that each of us comes to understand our own faith and experience of God via the narratives of our lives.

Preaching Everybody's Story

Nevertheless, it is valuable to provide a double-check or even corrective to the message we preach, simply to assure ourselves that the totality of the preached word does speak to the various life experiences of those in the pews. John Melloh, who taught preaching at the University of Notre Dame, proposed utilizing what he called the "Four Chair Theory." In practice, as the preacher nears the end of his preparation, he imagines four individuals of various ages, genders, and backgrounds seated before him. It is most helpful if the individuals are real persons known to the preacher. For example, it could be 75-year-old Carl, whose wife died six months ago; Cindy, who with her husband is delighting in the recent birth of their young daughter; Alex, who is 15 years old and has no desire to be in church but has come at the insistence of his parents; and Elizabeth, a 40-year-old single woman and who works as a nurse at the local hospital. Having nearly completed the homiletic preparation process, the preacher then imagines what he intends to say and imagines how these four diverse individuals will respond to his message. Will anything he intends to say touch each of these four individuals? Will the message have meaning for each of them? Will it describe how God is working in each of their lives? If so, then the preacher is ready to preach the message for that weekend. If not, he needs to go back to the drawing board, perhaps to add another example or two, perhaps to adjust the story, perhaps to tweak the way the message is presented.

If the task of the liturgical preacher is to describe how God is working in the world and what it is that God does, the preacher must describe God's actions in terms of the lives

---

[12] Barbara Hardy, "An Approach through Narrative," in *Towards a Poetics of Fiction: Essays from Novel, a Forum on Fiction, 1967–1976*, 31. Copyright © 1977, Indiana University Press. Reprinted with permission of Indiana University Press.

of those who are seated in the pews and not in terms of the preacher's own life. If the preacher describes what God has done in her own life, then the message becomes focused upon the preacher, and then it becomes a witness talk, something that can be valuable in another context such as a retreat. Liturgical preaching, however, has a different focus, directed toward the faithful gathered together. The *Homiletic Directory* cautions that "the time for the homily should not be taken up with the preacher's personal witness. There is no question that people can be deeply moved by personal stories, but the homily should express the faith of the Church, and not simply the preacher's own story." Nevertheless, the following paragraph does note that stories of personal witness "can be effective as *elements* of a good homily . . . If they serve the purpose of the homily, they are good; if they take the place of the homily, they are not."[13] On the other hand, for the preacher to name for herself what God has been doing in her own life can be a valuable part of the preparation process for the homily, for that can point her to look for those instances when God is doing the same thing in the lives of others.

In the novel *The Color Purple* by Alice Walker, the character Shug makes note of the difficulty of recognizing God in our lives, saying that God is inside of each of us, and can be found there if we look; even sometimes when we're not looking. Shug points out that it's hard times that help most of us to find God there.

Coming to see. Shug has it right. Sometimes we do stumble upon the seeing when we search for God, just because often enough it does feel more like a stumbling upon than a looking and finding. But most of the time it's as if we were blind and did not know we were blind. We need someone to point it out to us and describe what it is for which we should be looking. That is the task of the liturgical preacher.

 **The Preacher asks, "How would I describe God's activity in life during the past week?"**

---

[13] *Homiletic Directory,* par. 6 & 7.

CHAPTER 4

Challenging

Abba Anthony was a desert father who lived in the fourth century. One of his sage observations was that the time is coming when most people will be insane; when they see someone who is not insane, they will attack that person, saying, "You are insane because you are not like us." There are times when we prefer not to see, because if we could see we would then need to change. Sometimes the darkness is more comfortable. It can allow us to do what we want to do without any challenge.

In a classic *Calvin and Hobbes* comic strip, the oblivious Calvin that is in each of us does just that. Calvin acts on impulse lest conscience or common sense raise its voice of caution and challenge his instinct.

The Failure of Guilt

Like Calvin, we learn good behavior from experience and most often from the consequences of those experiences. It is after-the-fact wisdom. When toddlers are warned not to touch the stove because it is hot, eventually they learn to be cautious around stoves from testing it themselves and being burned. Somewhere in the human psyche is an instinct that compels us to test the advice we are given. While growing up we are taught to save our money, but only when we are broke do we realize the value of saving something for a rainy day. One of most parents' greatest fears is that a son or daughter will make some irreversible mistake that will affect the rest of their life. Thus parents warn their children against pregnancy before they are ready to be parents, or of the risks of driving recklessly lest an accident seriously harm them or one of their

passengers, or how the use of drugs can lead to lifelong dependency and struggle. Yet for some reason we seem to be willing to make our own mistakes as we experiment with life.

Adults are little different. We are advised of the dangers of smoking, of drinking and driving, of eating too much of the wrong kinds of foods. The benefits of eating fruits and vegetables, of exercising, of visiting the dentist on a regular basis, and on and on and on, are all explained to us. In so many areas of our lives we already know what we should and should not do. Yet there is little guarantee that we will heed all of the pieces of advice. Telling us one more time will not change our behavior. Not even discovering the negative consequences taking root in our lives will necessarily modify our behavior. In fact, research has shown that the least effective way to modify someone's behavior is to tell them what to do. It is simply not effective.

Why is it, then, that preachers are inclined to think that guilt motivates, that if they tell those in the pews one more time how to live the gospel, then they will change? All of us know we should forgive the aunt who has just insulted us, be patient on the phone with the lonely neighbor who needs to talk with someone and calls every day, love those who make obnoxious demands upon our time, and be kind to the office colleague who regularly takes the last cup of coffee without brewing another pot. Even the Christmas-and-Easter Catholic knows the Catholic Church's teachings on abortion, capital punishment, birth control, war, and euthanasia. Proclaiming such values one more time will do little to motivate anyone to alter their current practices or beliefs.

So what is the preacher to do to motivate the faithful toward living the gospel if telling them what to do is ineffective? Surely the wisdom of the tradition needs to be passed on. Surely that wisdom needs to be considered in making decisions for our lives. How does one challenge the listener?

Overhearing Goodness

The late Fred B. Craddock, professor of preaching at Emory University and an ordained minister of the Christian Church, wrote a book entitled *Overhearing the Gospel*.[14] In it he contended, rightly so, that if our behavior is directly confronted by another person, the normal response on our part is defensiveness. We are unable to "hear" the criticism or observation offered by the other person. If, on the other hand, we overhear that criticism in an indirect sort of way, as when it is not directly addressed to us, then we are more likely to take counsel with ourselves. For example, if you find yourself disagreeing with me as you read this chapter, and if you call me on the phone to tell me that what I am proposing is wrong and in error, chances are that I will become defensive and reply that you have totally missed my point, and that it is you who are in error. However, should I happen to overhear you offering that same opinion to someone else while you are unaware that I am listening, then I am more likely to think about your observations and take counsel with myself regarding the material in this chapter.

Craddock asserted that the same dynamic takes place when we listen to the scriptures being proclaimed in worship and prayer. The message is not directly addressed to each of us as if it were only us, but rather indirectly as it is proclaimed to everyone present and in fact to all believers. In other words, we overhear the gospel. Then our defenses are likely to be set aside. We are able to hear and be challenged. We are free to consider the message and take counsel with ourselves.

That same dynamic is at work when the preacher tells those in the pews what they should do. Defenses can arise. They may give themselves reasons why they cannot adopt the

---

[14] Fred B. Craddock, *Overhearing the Gospel* (Atlanta, GA: Chalice Press 2002).

behavior. They tell themselves that the preacher really does not understand their life situation and everything with which they must contend in the busyness of their lives. On the other hand, if the preacher tells a story of someone faced with a life situation that echoes the message being proclaimed, and if that story tells of the struggle and conflict, and if it goes on to describe the journey and motivation encountered, and how the conclusion brings greater wholeness even if not easily or without difficulty, in such a case the person in the pew is more likely to overhear the message and apply it to his or her own life situation without defensiveness or resistance. In other words, they take counsel with themselves.

Counsellors to Ourselves

The dynamic of motivating another person to take counsel with themselves in a reflective and faith-filled way has long been an ideal in the Catholic tradition. It is what we refer to as examining one's conscience and the need to be true to one's conscience. In addressing adults the practice of telling another how to live presumes that we know best concerning the correct and moral behavior in someone else's situation. To offer the tradition's wisdom is one thing. To insist that others translate that wisdom into their own personal circumstances is quite another. The fact of the matter is that the Catholic tradition has always counselled believers to follow their own conscience. Saint Thomas Aquinas, an esteemed doctor of the church, taught that "Conscience is more to be obeyed than authority imposed from the outside. By following a right conscience you not only do not incur sin but are also immune from sin, whatever superiors may say to the contrary. To act against one's conscience and to disobey a superior can both be sinful. Of the two the first is the worse since the dictate of conscience is more binding than the decree of external authority."[15] And Joseph Ratzinger (later Pope Benedict XVI) once wrote,

"Over the pope as the expression of the binding claim of ecclesiastical authority there still stands one's own conscience, which must be obeyed before all else, if necessary

---

[15] Thomas Aquinas, *De Veritate*, q.17, a.5.

even against the requirement of ecclesiastical authority. This emphasis on the individual, whose conscience confronts him with a supreme and ultimate tribunal, and one which in the last resort is beyond the claim of external social groups, even the official Church, also establishes a principle in opposition to increasing totalitarianism."[16]

As noted in the previous chapter, if the preacher is descriptive rather than prescriptive, if he or she is able to simply tell the story without concluding with the admonition, "Therefore we should . . . ," then the Spirit is more easily able to do its work and speak to the hearts of those who are listening. That takes some trust on the part of the preacher, who in all likelihood will never know whether the message was as challenging as hoped. It takes some trust that the Spirit is present. And it means that the preacher will not have the personal satisfaction that comes from having told someone what to do. But then that is not what preaching is about anyway.

Kathleen Norris is an American spiritual writer who lived for many years in Lemmon, South Dakota. She would go to parochial schools there as an artist-in-residence and teach children how to write poetry using the psalms as a model. This is how she describes one such occasion in her book *Amazing Grace.*

> Children who are picked on by their big brothers
> and sisters can be remarkably adept when it comes
> to writing cursing psalms, and I believe that the
> writing process offers them a safe haven in which
> to work through their desires for vengeance in
> a healthy way. Once a little boy wrote a poem
> called "The Monster Who Was Sorry." He began by
> admitting that he hates it when his father yells at
> him; his response in the poem is to throw his sister
> down the stairs, and then to wreck his room,

---

[16] Monograph by Joseph Ratzinger collected in *Commentary on the Documents of Vatican II, volume 5,* edited by Herbert Vorgrimler (New York: Herder and Herder, 1969), 134.

and finally to wreck the whole town. The poem concludes: "Then I sit in my messy house and say to myself, 'I shouldn't have done all that.' "[17]

How do we enable people to have that sort of honesty with themselves? Notably, it is in the solitude amid the messiness of his house that the boy comes face to face with what he has done. It is there that he says to himself, "I shouldn't have done all that." In much the same way, if the preacher has created the space for the persons in the pew to take counsel with themselves, if the preacher has allowed those persons of faith to overhear their own life in the story told, then it might be in the silence following the homily, and perhaps in the reflective silence beyond the liturgy itself, that they find themselves sitting with the messiness of their real selves—not with their public selves, not with the selves they wish they were, not with their pretend selves, but with their real selves as they truly are.

 **The Prophet asks, "What aspects of the past week were challenges for me? For parishioners? For the local or national communities? When did we respond with grace?"**

---

[17] Kathleen Norris, *Amazing Grace: A Vocabulary of Faith* (New York: Riverhead Books, 1998), 69–70. Copyright © 1998, Kathleen Norris, published by The Berkley Publishing Group, a Division of Penguin Group (USA), Inc. Used by permission.

CHAPTER 5

Only One Message

"If there is mist in the pulpit, there will be fog in the pews." It is an apt quip. If the preacher is unsure what his or her message is, surely those who listen will not know what the preacher is trying to say.

Bishop Ken Untener wrote a book for preachers entitled *Preaching Better.* It is a collection of pastoral thoughts and reflections on effective preaching. A part of each chapter is what he calls "Feedback from the Folks." This is some of the feedback he recounts in his chapter on "Preparing a Homily: Just One Pearl . . . But of Great Price."

- Make just one point, and let us think about it.

- She starts out giving a good homily, but then goes on and tries to say too much.

- Don't forget that there will be other Sundays. You'll get a chance to say more.

- You don't follow scotch with gin and then have some bourbon. They might all be the very best, but one ruins the other.

- He wanders from one idea to another—no one central point that you can take home.

- He gets his point across and then starts repeating it and bringing in all kinds of other things.[18]

Clearly these folks in the pews listen to the preaching and are interested in the message and in understanding it. We who preach have a great responsibility to nourish and sustain their faith by proclaiming the word of God in ways that do just that.

One Message at a Time

The simplest way to be clear in one's homily is to have only one message. If the preacher offers a few unrelated but pointed comments on each of the scripture readings, that tends to muddy the waters. Most often all three readings have not been chosen to harmonize with each other. Even the first and third readings are not always in harmony, as at times during the Easter season. Exegetical commentary in the context of the homily also tends to unmoor the message, unless of course such commentary is necessary to give direction and light to the message. Finally, scattered thoughts on the scriptures of the day tend to move no one toward remembering any of the ideas, even if the preacher's hope is that something will stick if enough is thrown at the wall. It seldom does. There is too much to remember, so nothing is remembered.

In *The Joy of the Gospel* Pope Francis warns preachers about saying too much or preaching a message that has little or no focus. It only ends up being confusing.

> But our own aim is not to understand every little detail of a text; our most important goal is to discover its principal message, the message which gives structure and unity to the text. If the preacher does not make this effort, his preaching will quite likely have neither unity nor order; what he has to say will be a mere accumulation of various disjointed ideas incapable of inspiring others.[19]

---

[18] Ken Untener, *Preaching Better: Practical Suggestions for Homilists*, 44. Copyright © 1999, Most Reverend Kenneth Untener, published by Paulist Press. Used with permission of Paulist Press.

[19] Pope Francis, The Joy of the Gospel: *Evangelii gaudium*, Apostolic Exhortation. Vatican City: *Libreria Editrice Vaticana*, 2013, par. 147.

The greatest risk for a preacher is that he becomes so accustomed to his own language that he thinks that everyone else naturally understands and uses it . . . Simplicity and clarity are two different things. Our language may be simple but our preaching not very clear. It can end up being incomprehensible because it is disorganized, lacks logical progression or tries to deal with too many things at one time.[20]

In Six Words or Less

To preach with clarity it is important that the preacher know what he wishes to communicate; in other words, he must know his own message. Yet it might be that the preacher is unsure himself. An effective way of clarifying one's message is to state it in a sentence, subject–verb–object, and to state it in six words or less. To be sure, there is nothing magical about the number six. If you wish, make it seven words or less, or eight words. But make the message brief and direct: subject–verb–object. Thus "Faith" is not a message. It is a topic, as is also "The Fragility of Faith." On the other hand, "God dismantles and rebuilds faith" is a message about God's activity. So too is "God sows seeds of faith." That also is a message.

In each of the two examples, notice that God is the subject of the sentence. If a homily is about pointing to where God is doing today what God did then, then it is helpful to craft the message in terms of God as the subject of the sentence. It is also a corrective that prevents us from slipping into telling people what they should do. It crafts the message as a declarative sentence rather than an imperative. And finally, it assures us that we will talk about God or about Jesus or about the Spirit. It can become too easy to slip into commentary about a recent film the preacher has seen or about "Dear Abby" or about political commentary. The point is not that those materials are off-limits in a homily, but rather that they are not the subject of the homily. God is the subject, even though such references can help us see where God is and what God is doing in our lives.

---

[20] *Evangelii gaudium*; par. 158.

Finding a Fresh Message

At some point in the preparation process the preacher needs to settle upon the message that he or she wishes to preach. As most preachers have come to realize, it is valuable to begin early in the week. Here is one helpful process. On the first reading of each text, circle or underline the words or phrases that intrigue or jump out at you for whatever reason. Then name what is going on in your own life that might make you take particular note of that word or phrase. What is going on in your own life may or may not have anything to do with the ultimate message you will preach, or with God and faith, or even with anything noteworthy. That is unimportant. What you are doing at this point is simply "mining" the texts, surfacing ideas and images that may lead to something worthwhile later on. Having done this, then do the exegesis of the text and see if that in any way sheds light upon the earlier personal exploration you have done. Again, it may or may not, but through it all the juices of what is going on in life begin to come to the surface. Finally, do you see any of this going on in the lives of others, in the Church, or in the local or national community?

Somewhere in the process it is good to begin naming what each text is saying about what God does. That is not always a simple task, particularly when the text is an admonition or directive. Yet somewhere in all of that is God's activity in our lives, or at least advice on how to take note of God's activity. It is also helpful to name how each text highlights three different activities of God, three possible and different messages. Why three? Because the first idea that surfaces is most often going to be the obvious message. For example, the story of the Prodigal Son tells us that God forgives. We all know that. We have heard that message before. So has everyone else. Thus it would be more difficult to craft from that idea a message that is engaging and one that offers a fresh insight into how God works in our lives. Involving ourselves in the work of mining three messages for each text forces us to deeper prayer and reflection. It also provides the opportunity for a greater variety of messages from which to choose, as well as the possibility of discovering previously unrecognized connections among the three texts. The point in all of this is that however we move through the scripture texts of the day, sooner or later it is crucial that we decide in a very intentional way just what we want to preach about how God works in our lives.

To Write or Not to Write

One more point related to focusing on only one message: Some have recommended that writing out one's homily can help give it clarity and focus. That may be true, but writing is not always necessary. Allow me to explain. The value of writing out a homily may depend upon whether or not one is an extrovert or an introvert on the Myers-Briggs personality scale. Those acquainted with the Myers-Briggs indicators understand that extroverts are those who clarify their thinking on a subject by talking it through aloud. Introverts, on the other hand, are those who clarify their thinking by going off to some quiet corner and sorting it out in their heads before they can talk about a topic. These personality types represent different ways of dealing with information. My suspicion is that extroverts particularly benefit from writing out a homily. For them it is another way of "speaking" it out, and the process of writing brings clarity and focus to their thoughts. Introverts, however, do not seem to benefit as much from writing out what they want to say simply because their normal process of bringing order and focus to their thoughts is done before they open their mouths. Neither personality trait is good or bad. It is simply the way we are wired, and so it is helpful to know which we are.

While writing out a homily can certainly have definite benefits, there is also a drawback for some individuals. Most people speak and write with two different styles. We tend to speak more casually and we tend to write more formally. If a homily is written out with more formal expressions and phrases, it may also be more artistically descriptive and engaging. Then the inclination will be to preach the way it has been written simply because we like the way the message has been expressed. But what may be lost is the spontaneity and energy of the preacher when the message flows through his or her personality in a more natural way of conversation and communication.

In the end, some may find it more effective to focus their preaching by writing it out first and thus bringing clarity. Others may find their preaching more effective if they do not write out their homily ahead of time and thus speak with more energy and natural conviction. As the sage has said, "Know thyself."

 **The Preacher asks, "What one aspect of God's movement in human life as told in this Sunday's scriptures do I want to share with the faithful who gather? What will my message be in six words or less?"**

The Poet asks, "If the past week were a novel of God's movement in life, what title would I give it?"

CHAPTER 6

Appeals to Our Hearts

Prose is about something, but poetry is about what can't be said. Why do people turn to poetry when all of a sudden the Twin Towers get hit, or when their marriage breaks up, or when the person they love most in the world drops dead in the same room? Because they can't say it. They can't say it at all, and they want something that addresses what can't be said.[21]

—W.S. Merwin

Preaching is really the poetry of faith. People want someone to say what faith is about, what God is about, because they feel that faith is something that can't be said. No one seems to know how, so we look to the preacher.

The use of a metaphor or an image is much more than simply a nice thing to include in our preaching. When it is

---

[21] W.S. Merwin, quoted in Academy of Achievement. "W.S. Merwin Interview—Academy of Achievement." Last modified July 3, 2008. Accessed January 19, 2016. http://www.achievement.org/autodoc/page/mer0int-1.

well chosen and well crafted it can speak to another person's most deeply held beliefs. Once each month for a number of years now I have been writing a reflection on the Sunday scriptures for the local Catholic newspaper. In one such reflection I referred to the well-known poem "Footprints in the Sand." I mentioned that personally I did not care for the poem, perhaps because it had become overused, perhaps because I thought it was trite, or perhaps it simply did not speak something new to me. At any rate, I wrote that I did not care for it even though I was aware that for many people it was a favorite. Following my reflection's publication in that week's issue, I received a strongly worded letter from someone chiding me for such insensitivity to the ways of God in human life. Could it possibly be, the person wondered, that I thought one could go through life without God's assistance? Surely I was lacking in faith. "Footprints in the Sand" had clearly become a sacred image for that person, as treasured perhaps as an image of the Sacred Heart or an image of the Madonna and Child. Metaphors and creative images have the power to speak to the deepest corners of our faith life. They appeal to our hearts.

Using Metaphors

Metaphors work by finding a common denominator and then expanding it to include the whole. They speak mostly in what they do not say outright; they say more than what they seem to say. Metaphors intrigue and engage our imaginations. That is why we tend to remember them. I would like to offer two examples, each of them a different kind of metaphor.

Metaphor #1. In so many ways life is a box of crayons, all with their tips so perfectly pointed and arranged in rows of matched and tinted hues. Each color seems so eager to make its mark, brilliant or shy or somber or faint, like a wistful touch of some bygone season. There is something about a brand new box of forty-eight crayons, something that makes you want to pause a bit in awe and reverence. Burnt sienna, magenta, turquoise, mahogany, apricot, salmon, periwinkle, lemon—the names themselves make you want to pull them out of the box and start coloring. They are simply waiting to be put to use.

Each color seems to hold a promise, if only you knew how to use it, how to put it onto the paper so that it comes alive.

Obviously life is not really a box of crayons, and yet in so many ways it is. That is the power of metaphor.

Metaphor #2. This year's eighth-graders are rushing toward the wilds of impending high school. For the most part they have spent this last year of grade school life like every other class of parish eighth-graders, sheepishly trying to be like everyone else and looking for ways to suppress what makes them different. Yet despite their instincts to blend into the teenage ensemble,they've already begun to strike their own chords. Steven dreams of being a financial analyst, Shelly a pediatrician, Gabby a psychologist, Emily a third grade teacher, Liz M. an art teacher, Liz P. a doctor, and both Jerome and Micah physical therapists. There is much time for all of that to change and change again. Yet something in each of them, call it God's Spirit, is bringing their own gifts to the surface and eventually to fruition.

These two metaphors or images, the box of crayons and the graduating class of eighth-graders, are certainly very different realities, and yet they are quite similar. It could be said that the box of crayons readily describes the class of graduating eighth-graders, each student with a differently colored personality tinged with God's Spirit. Yet if life is a box of crayons, then it is also a box of Spirit, so many gifts of God enfleshed in so many different individuals, each of them revealing on the canvas of life a different color, a different hue.

Preachers who are able to utilize images are able to engage the imaginations of those who listen to them. They capture interest with an image and hold on to that interest as they develop its meaning with real-life examples.

In a sense, both of our examples are metaphors. The first, the image of life as a box of crayons is **metaphor of illustration.** It compares one reality with another, and yet it does not equate the two realities. A box of crayons and life are two separate realities. One is used to illustrate the other.

The second, the class of eighth-graders, is a **metaphor of participation.** It compares a moment in life with the gift of God's Spirit to each individual. In fact it equates the two, in contrast to what happens when we compare life to a box of crayons, which are not equated, only compared. In the instance of the class of eighth-graders, they are compared and also equated with our understanding of how the Holy Spirit moves and works in our lives. Actually, the **metaphor of participation** is doing what a homily does. In this instance the metaphor points to how and where God is doing today what God did back then in the stories of the scriptures. It is an example of God participating in life and life participating in God.

Allow me to use another example of the two uses of the term *metaphor*. No doubt you have heard the phrase "You are the sunshine of my life." Obviously the person addressed is not literally sunshine. It is a descriptive image, and as such it is a metaphor of illustration applied to a specific person. By comparison, if someone should say, "When you fold the laundry for me and empty the dishwasher, that makes my day so much easier. It brightens my day," that then becomes a metaphor of participation. It is the actual reality pointed to by the phrase "You are the sunshine of my life."

When preaching, every homily should utilize a **metaphor of participation,** which is to say every homily should employ an example of God moving in human life. It makes real the presence of God in our world. When employing a metaphor of **illustration** as well, the homily takes on another dimension that engages the imagination and interest of the listener. The homily is enriched in a way that allows the listeners to apply the message in terms of their own experiences.

Finding an Image

Yet how does the preacher tap into such images? The fact is that images like these are all around us. All we need do is observe and reflect. One definition of creativity is the ability to relate two seemingly disparate realities. Certainly preaching seeks to do that—to relate the events of life and the activity of God. Faith is the lens by which we see.

Seeking images that will echo the faith-life of those who listen is also a kind of creativity. Take this example from the poetry of Stanley Kunitz. Occasionally a songwriter will remark how a few bars of music gave birth to an entire song, or an artist will explain how the way light struck an object or part of a landscape became the inspiration for a painting. Poet Stanley Kunitz made the same comment about a phrase he heard in a dream. "Live in the layers / not on the litter." He explained that the meaning of the two lines was initially confusing for him, but eventually they became the inspiration for a poem.

> I have walked through many lives,
> some of them my own,
> and I am not who I was,
> though some principle of being
> abides, from which I struggle
> not to stray . . .
> In my darkest night,
> when the moon was covered
> and I roamed through wreckage,
> a nimbus-clouded voice
> directed me:
> "Live in the layers,
> not in the litter."[22]

For him the image came to suggest the need to enter into the depths of life, messy as that could be. Though it risked having the very marrow of his bones being sucked away, the risk was preferable, even necessary, he posited, rather than living among the litter and clutter found on the distracting surface of life. It is in the layers that one contends with darkness and light, with love and indifference, with meaning and abandonment.

There is something transcendent about beauty, whether that of a single rose, the palette of color on a wooded autumn path, or a haunting melody played upon a flute. Such transcendence is not exactly otherworldly, but is a quality of something or someone that draws us into a sense of wonder and awe—a glimpse of the divine, some would say. Images, whether spoken or written, can have that same impact as well. If God is love, if God is peace, if God is joy, then God is also beauty.

---

[22] Excerpted from Stanley Kunitz, "The Layers," from *The Collected Poems* by Stanley Kunitz. Used by permission of W.W. Norton & Company, Inc.

In *The Joy of the Gospel* Pope Francis himself encourages us to use images in our preaching.

One of the most important things is to learn how to use images in preaching, how to appeal to imagery. Sometimes examples are used to clarify a certain point, but these examples usually appeal only to the mind; images, on the other hand, help people better to appreciate and accept the message we wish to communicate. An attractive image makes the message seem familiar, close to home, practical and related to everyday life. A successful image can make people savour the message, awaken a desire and move the will toward the Gospel.[23]

Tapping into Creativity

Walter Burghardt was a Jesuit scholar and well-known preacher in the latter days of the twentieth century. He once explained how he would tap into the creative juices that fed his preaching by listening to Beethoven's Fifth Symphony blasting from his stereo. He found that by immersing himself in creativity, he would find the creative spirit coming to the surface in himself. One preacher told me that he reads poetry toward that same end. Another goes to the art museum and sits before a beautiful painting. Another listens to country western music. Another goes for a walk in the woods. Whatever it is that stirs the muse of creativity within your own spirit, immerse yourself in it. It stirs its power in you.

Another way to bring the use of images to your preaching is by incorporating an image into the six-word statement of your message. If the message is articulated as "subject–verb–object" with God as the subject, then utilizing a verb that states the message poetically can engage the listener's imagination and interest as well. Think of the forcefulness of the Portuguese proverb "God writes straight with crooked lines." Be creative and imaginative. Instead of "God is present in all we do," consider "God drizzles life all over us" or "God haunts our haunts." Instead of "God forgives," consider "God teases us into new life" or "God unravels our sin." Finding a

---

[23] *Evangelii gaudium*, par. 157.

poetic image for the message can also inspire new ways for the preacher to convey the activity of God and give the preacher new eyes with which to see during the process of preparation.

Here are some verbs suggesting different ways to articulate how God acts in our world. They might open a new perspective on God's activity.

GOD . . .

balances	groans	seals
bangs	grooms	seduces
bleeds	harvests	seeps
bottles up	haunts	shrinks
breaches	hollows	simmers
bridges	hints at	sinks
bubbles up	hunts	skates
carves	inflates	sneaks
charges	intimidates	spars
collapses	jumps	spills
cools	knocks	splits
cracks	overturns	sprints
crumbles	parades	straddles
dances	plants	stretches
dreams	prospects (as in mining)	stuns
dresses	revels	tattoos
drizzles	saves (as in stamps)	teases
edges	scatters	traps
escapes	scavenges	unravels
feuds	scours	veils
floods	scribbles	weaves
goes into debt		

A few years ago I was on a retreat in northern Wisconsin. In the woods on the property there were paths marked by cairns, each one fifty yards or so beyond the one before. Someone had taken the time and made the effort to balance one stone upon another, each held in place by that one thread of instinct called gravity than ran through the very center of the column and kept it from toppling. The harmony of each one, five or six stones one atop another, made me stand in wonder before their simplicity and the mystery of their balance that defied the logic that assumed they should fall. The use of an appropriate metaphor or image can be such a thread holding the entire homily together, balancing it in such a way that we listen and understand with wonder how life is also threaded with God.

 **The Poet asks, "Out of my prayer with these texts, what has touched my heart and excited me about God's presence? What image or picture describes that excitement?"**

CHAPTER 7

Appeals to Our Minds

The poet Wallace Stevens once observed, "Perhaps the truth depends on a walk around the lake."[24] You and I go through life looking for the truth of how to live our lives, a truth that so often seems just beyond our grasp. A walk around the lake might reveal it to us. So might the right book or a conversation with a friend, but so too might the preacher. In fact, that is largely what we want from the one who stands up and preaches—not so much to tell us what to do but to shed light on how it is with our lives, how God is present even when it does not always seem so to us, and how we might negotiate the maze in which we find ourselves. We would like to hear some wisdom—not some theology but some wisdom.

Frederick Buechner describes what it is like as we sit down after the proclamation of the Gospel with a fragile expectation and hope:

---

[24] Excerpted from Wallace Stevens, "Notes Toward a Supreme Fiction" in *The Collected Poems of Wallace Stevens* (New York: Vintage Books, 1990), 386.

The preacher pulls the little cord that turns on the lectern light and deals out his note cards like a riverboat gambler. The stakes have never been higher. Two minutes from now he may have lost his listeners completely to their own thoughts, but at this minute he has them in the palm of his hand. The silence in the shabby church is deafening because everybody is listening to it. Everybody is listening including even himself. Everybody knows the kind of things he has told them before and not told them, but who knows what this time, out of the silence, he will tell them?[25]

This is an awesome, even frightening, expectation for the preacher to realize that those who sit before him are hoping for some sort of beacon by which they might navigate their lives. Most likely they would settle for a little candlelight if it would help them make their way in the darkness lest they trip over their own clutter.

Four Kinds of Preaching

In recent years there has been much discussion and much written about catechetical preaching and whether or not it should take the place of the homily in our liturgical gatherings. While it is true that there is a real need among many lay persons for an understanding of the teachings of our tradition, that is not what they tell us they come looking for in the homilies they hear. Nor would catechetical preaching be able to bring much depth or understanding to any theological topic in the span of a ten-minute presentation, to say nothing about whether or not it would be remembered. Too readily, then, our preaching would simply devolve into telling people what to believe.

Some years ago the U.S. Catholic Bishops' Committee on Priestly Life and Ministry published *Fulfilled in Your Hearing,*[26]

---

[25] Frederick Buechner, *Telling the Truth: The Gospel as Tragedy, Comedy, and Fairy Tale* (New York: Harper & Row, 1977), 23. Copyright © 1977 by Frederick Buechner. Reprinted courtesy of HarperCollins Publishers.

[26] Bishops' Committee on Priestly Life and Ministry, *Fulfilled in Your Hearing: The Homily in the Sunday Assembly* (Washington, DC: United States Conference of Catholic Bishops, 1982).

a document on preaching in today's world. The document points to four different kinds of preaching. **Pre-evangelization** seeks to instill an initial interest in the gospel. It talks about life and love and joy and friendship. It is the kind of preaching we do with pre-teens or young teens, hoping that they might seek to know more about what Jesus has to say. The goal of **Evangelization** is initial conversion. While conversion is ultimately a lifelong journey, evangelization preaches Christ crucified that we might turn our lives over to the Lord Jesus and seek to live in his image and likeness. Street-corner preaching and televangelism are good examples. **Catechetics** seeks to pass on the tradition, to instill an understanding of the truths of the Christian faith. Moralizing, or preaching the dangers and pitfalls of sin, is a kind of catechetical preaching. Finally, the **Homily** preaches the *kerygma*, the passion, death, and resurrection of the Lord Jesus as it continues to unfold in our present day. It seeks to bring us to wonder and awe over how God moves in our world. There may be occasions when a preacher chooses to offer catechetical preaching, and in such an instance he or she should simply understand that it is not a homily. Keeping in mind these four different kinds of preaching can be helpful to understanding what it is we do when we step into the pulpit.

Preaching the Path to Faith

In The Joy of the Gospel (*Evangelii gaudium*) Pope Francis warns that "preaching which would be purely moralistic or doctrinaire, or one which turns into a lecture on biblical exegesis, detracts from this heart-to-heart communication which takes place in the homily."[27] On his 2013 trip to Brazil Pope Francis continually restated that fact: it is not through intellectual understanding that people come to faith. "Perhaps we have reduced our way of speaking about mystery to rational explanations," he told the assembled bishops, "but for ordinary people the mystery enters through the heart. Only the beauty of

---

[27] *Evangelii gaudium*, par. 142.

God can attract . . . God's way is through enticement, allure."[28] Later on he described the work of the Church in much the same way. "The results of our pastoral work do not depend on a wealth of resources, but on the creativity of love . . . At times we lose people because they don't understand what we are saying, because we have forgotten the language of simplicity and import an intellectualism foreign to our people."[29]

Pope Francis seems to be calling for a preaching that offers the wisdom of Jesus by which we can make our way through life. Most recently, in *The Joy of the Gospel,* Francis quoted Pope John Paul II as he reiterated that same message:

> It is worth remembering that "the liturgical proclamation of the word of God, especially in the Eucharistic assembly, is not so much a time for meditation and catechesis as a dialogue between God and his people, a dialogue in which the great deeds of salvation are proclaimed and the demands of the covenant are continually restated." The homily has special importance due to its Eucharistic context: it surpasses all forms of catechesis as the supreme moment in the dialogue between God and his people which leads up to sacramental communion. The homily takes up once more the dialogue which the Lord has already established with his people.[30]

The *Homiletic Directory* summarizes the wisdom of Popes Francis and John Paul II when it advises that the homily "is not a sermon on an abstract topic . . . Nor is the homily simply an exercise in biblical exegesis . . . the homilist is called to proclaim how God's word is being fulfilled here and now. Next, the homily is not catechetical instruction, even if catechesis is an important dimension of the homily. As with biblical exegesis, there is not the time to do this properly."[31]

There is a difference between the truths of theology and the

---

[28] Address of Pope Francis, Apostolic Journey to Rio de Janeiro on the Occasion of the XXVIII World Youth Day, Meeting with the Bishops of Brazil, July 28, 2013. Vatican City: *Libreria Editrice Vaticana,* 2013.

[29] Ibid.

[30] *Evangelii gaudium,* par. 137.

[31] *Homiletic Directory,* par. 6.

spirituality of our journey. The former leads to understanding, the latter to wisdom and an encounter with the Lord Jesus. That is why we are advised to preach a homily and not theology. On the other hand, effective preaching flows out of a healthy and well-grounded theology. None of this implies that a homily may not contain theology, but only that the communication of theology or catechetics is not the goal or purpose of the homily.

Mining the One Idea

So if those who sit before us in the pews come seeking a message that appeals not only to their hearts but also to their minds, how might we preach without in the end preaching theology? A fair question. The USCCB document on preaching, *Preaching the Mystery of Faith,* published in 2013, encourages us to use "the technique of *lectio divina,* which Pope Benedict XVI has recommended to all believers, [by which] we are able to absorb more deeply the breathtaking beauty and power of the Scriptures (see *Verbum Domini,* nos. 86–87). This venerable method of approaching the Scriptures, the pope observes, begins with a prayerful reading of the biblical text, then a meditation on its message, followed by a prayerful response on our part concerning what the Lord may ask of us through this biblical passage, and finally, contemplation of what conversion of heart and mind will be necessary to bring the message of the word to action in our lives and those of others."[32]

Again, Pope Francis reminds us of the value of *lectio divina* in preparation for our liturgical preaching.

> It consists of reading God's word in a moment of prayer and allowing it to enlighten and renew us. This prayerful reading of the Bible is not something separate from the study undertaken by the preacher to ascertain the central message of the text; on the contrary, it should begin with that study and then go on to discern how that same message speaks to his own life.

---

[32] *Preaching the Mystery of Faith,* 9.

In the presence of God, during a recollected reading of the text, it is good to ask, for example: "Lord, what does this text say *to me?* What is it about my life that you want to change by this text? What troubles me about this text? Why am I not interested in this? Or perhaps: What do I find pleasant in this text? What is it about this word that moves me? What attracts me? Why does it attract me?"[33]

Anyone who has ever prepared to preach knows well that we preach first to ourselves before we ever stand before the community. The insights and challenges we find through our prayer become, then, the lenses through which we observe how those same dynamics are taking place in the lives of others. As noted earlier, this is not to suggest that we should preach our own stories, for that would put the focus upon us rather than on those who listen, and thus it would become a witness talk. However, our own stories become a good starting point in the process of preparation and a source of insight into God's activity in life.

Another way of tapping into the vein of wisdom can be the practice of meeting with small groups of parishioners to mine the scriptures for the coming weekend. Many preachers make use of this process, a kind of combination of bible study of the text and group *lectio divina*. Such a gathering can ground the preacher in the lives of those to whom he will be preaching. It can name their joys and sorrows, difficulties and successes, hopes and disappointments. A weekly meeting of parishioners to explore the scriptures can assure the preacher that he is addressing the spiritual and life needs of his people, lest he resort to pious platitudes or theological window dressing that have little value or substance.

Yet another source for finding something worthwhile to say in our preaching comes from the reading we do. Many years ago another priest shared with me his observation that he found himself always preaching what he had been reading. Over and over again I have found that to be true. Whenever I find myself with nothing to say on a particular weekend, I realize that I have not been reading. This does not necessarily mean reading theology or spirituality, though it may mean

---

[33] *Evangelii gaudium,* par. 152, 153.

that, but also novels or social commentary or poetry or news magazines or watching films—anything that brings new insight and understanding into our own lives. As noted earlier, this does not mean that we preach this material as our message. Always we are about preaching the gospel, but we point to these reflections of life as the contemporary expressions of what the gospel speaks. Such material echoes and reflects the gospel's wisdom and light. If we do not read often, we will find that we have little new to say. The nuggets of our own continual learning find their way into our preaching.

Some time ago H. Jackson Brown Jr. published listings of what people had learned in life. He called them *Live and Learn and Pass It On.* Below are a few such tidbits from his second volume.[34] They are a kind of perception that seems to embody the wisdom that Jesus brought to us long before. None of this supplants the gospel message, but it can be a way of rephrasing it in the everyday language of the people in the pews.

One such insight comes from someone who was 57 years old. "I've learned that everyone wants to live on the top of the mountain, but all the happiness and growth occurs while you're climbing it" (page 67). It seems to echo the wisdom of Jesus: "Whoever wishes to come after me must deny himself, take up his cross, and follow me. For whoever wishes to save his life will lose it, but whoever loses his life for my sake will find it" (Matthew 16:24–25).

Another came from someone who was 32 at the time. "I've learned that just because someone doesn't love you the way you want them to doesn't mean they don't love you with all they have" (page 52). It certainly sheds new light on the teaching of Jesus that we love our neighbor as ourselves (Mark 12:31).

Someone at age 44 passed on this discovery, "I've learned that I was part of the mess. Both children are gone, and there are still crumbs on the kitchen counter and floor" (page 63). It may very well be another way of considering that all of us who seek the kingdom are a mixture of wheat and weeds in the field of our lives (Matthew 13:24–30).

---

[34] H. Jackson Brown Jr., *Live and Learn and Pass It On, Volume II: People Ages 5 to 95 Share What They've Discovered About Life, Love, and Other Good Stuff*, copyright © 1995 by H. Jackson Brown, Jr. All rights reserved. Used by permission.

In the end we all come and sit before the word of God in search of some wisdom, and it is the task of the preacher to interpret that wisdom for us in today's language. It's not book learning that we seek when we listen to someone preach. It is a kind of wisdom, however, that appeals to our minds, so when we walk down the aisle and out into life at the end of our gathering, we may have something from God's word to think about.

 **The Poet asks, "As a result of my prayer with these scriptures, what wisdom or insight into God's presence have I realized that I was not aware of a week ago?"**

CHAPTER 8

Tells the Story of the Community

In a scene in the play *Saint Joan* by George Bernard Shaw, Joan explains to Robert de Baudricourt how she knows what God wants of her. Robert doubts her, or perhaps is confused by her, and so she explains, "I hear voices telling me what to do. They come from God." Robert insists, "They come from your imagination." "Of course," replies Joan. "That is how the messages of God come to us." [35]

There are those in this life who do seem to hear different voices, not because they are not in touch with reality, but precisely because they seem to be more in tune with all that is going on, more so than the rest of us. They hear the voices of the poor as well as those of the wealthy, of both the learned and the simple, of the young and of the aged. They pick up the rhythms of the human heart as well as the rhythms at the heart of the community. They do what poets do. They give voice to what they hear.

---

[35] George Bernard Shaw, *Saint Joan*, Act I.

Preachers can and should be the poets of the faith community and for the faith community. If they are not, who will provide that voice? We need someone to see beneath the surface of life's busyness and tell God's story taking place in the community—both the national community and the local one. To say that the preacher serves as the poet of the faith community is really another way of saying that the preacher serves as the spiritual director of the community, the one who sees the rhythms of God and hears the voices of God in our communal lives and then speaks what he or she hears.

Telling the community's story, however, will often lead to recognizing the failings of the community, much as we recognize our own individual pitfalls. Indeed, there is sufficient communal sin of which to take note. Mohandas Gandhi once outlined what he considered to be the greatest dangers to society. They have come to be called the "Seven Social Sins."

- Politics without Principle
- Wealth without Work
- Pleasure without Conscience
- Knowledge without Character
- Commerce without Morality
- Science without Humanity
- Worship without Sacrifice

Surely these are present in our midst, yet preaching about their evils quickly seems to drift into moralizing and guilt. "This is what we should do . . . This is what we as a society must overcome . . . If we as a society are to live the gospel, we must . . ." So parishioners leave our assemblies feeling rather guilty for not living the gospel while at the same time not knowing what anyone can do in the face of such mammoth tasks. As *Preaching the Mystery of Faith* points out, "For this reason many teachers of homiletics warn, quite legitimately, against 'moralizing' homilies, which harp excessively or exclusively on sin and its dangers. But when the offer of grace is also clear and presented with pastoral sensitivity, the recipient of that grace wants to change and wants to know what the new life in Christ looks like concretely."[36]

So how then can one preach the values of justice for our society in a constructive way, since ignoring them should not be an option? Earlier in our consideration of effective preaching, preachers were urged to be descriptive rather than prescriptive. If we are told what to do, most of us become defensive, guilt-ridden, overwhelmed, and usually inactive. However, if we see how and where someone is living out such values, God's Spirit seems to become active in us, instilling a desire to live in such ways ourselves. The reality is that those who sit in the pews of our churches do try to be good people who live out the gospel.

Seven Major Themes of Catholic Social Teaching

The United States Conference of Catholic Bishops has articulated seven major themes of Catholic social teaching.[37] Here is a summary of each of those seven themes, followed by my own examples of instances in which our faith communities are valuing them, addressing them, and bringing them to fruition in the comings and goings of community life. Some have been institutionalized in the larger civic community. Others occur in the rhythms of parish life. By simply pointing this out in the context of preaching the gospel, over the course of the year we will in effect be preaching the values of social justice, and furthermore we will be describing rather than prescribing. We will be celebrating the gospel being lived rather than commiserating over our sinfulness. That is surely more hopeful.

---

[36] *Preaching the Mystery of Faith,* 11.

[37] The descriptions of the seven major themes of Catholic Social Teaching presented here are adapted from *Sharing Catholic Social Teaching— Challenges and Directions, Reflections of the U.S. Catholic Bishops,* copyright © 1998, United States Conference of Catholic Bishops, Washington, DC. Used with permission. All rights reserved.

Life and Dignity of the Human Person

Our belief in the sanctity of human life and the inherent dignity of the human person is the foundation of all the principles of our social teaching. We believe that every person is precious, that people are more important than things, and that the measure of every institution is whether it threatens or enhances the life and dignity of the human person.

A faith community values this when . . .

- parishioners visit those in nursing homes and hospitals to pray with them and bring them the Eucharist.

- parishioners are actively involved in prison ministry.

- the parish is aware of the seamless garment of life.

- there is education to protect children from sexual abuse.

- support groups for addicted individuals are offered in the community.

Call to Family, Community, and Participation

Our tradition proclaims that the person is not only sacred but also social. How we organize our society—in economics and politics, in law and policy—directly affects human dignity and the capacity of individuals to grow in community. The family is the central social institution that must be supported and strengthened, not undermined. We believe people have a right and a duty to participate in society, seeking together the common good and well-being of all, especially those who are poor and vulnerable. The role of government and other institutions is to protect and promote the common good.

A faith community values this when . . .

- it celebrates the feast of the Holy Family.

- it offers blessings on Mother's Day and Father's Day.

- it celebrates marriages and baptisms and wedding anniversaries.

- it promotes voter education.

- the larger community celebrates the Fourth of July.

- schools honor grandparents with a Grandparents' Day.

Rights and Responsibilities

The Catholic tradition teaches that human dignity can be protected and a healthy community can be achieved only if human rights are protected and responsibilities are met. Every person has a fundamental right to life and a right to those things required for a decent human life. Corresponding to these rights are duties and responsibilities—to one another, to our families, and to the larger society.

A faith community values this when . . .

- it reminds and encourages parishioners to vote.

- it supports universal health care.

- it seeks to improve the quality of public education.

- it promotes the right to life.

Option for the Poor and Vulnerable

Catholic teaching proclaims that a basic moral test is how our most vulnerable members are faring. In a society marred by deepening divisions between rich and poor, our tradition instructs us to put the needs of those who are poor and vulnerable first.

A faith community values this when . . .

- it supports or provides food banks for those in need.

- parishioners participate in local meal programs.

- it sponsors a chapter of the St. Vincent de Paul Society.

- Christmas gifts are gathered during the season of Advent for those in need.

- it participates in the annual Campaign for Human Development collection.

The Dignity of Work and the Rights of Workers

We believe that the economy must serve people, not the other way around. Work is more than a way to make a living; it is a form of continuing participation in God's creation. If the dignity of work is to be protected, then the basic rights of workers must be respected—the right to productive work, to decent and fair wages, to organize and join unions, to private property, and to economic initiative.

A faith community values this when . . .

- it provides support groups for those who are unemployed.

- it provides just and equitable wages for staffs and teachers.

- it prays for an honest minimum wage.

- it celebrates Labor Day with the civic community.

Solidarity

Our culture is tempted to turn inward, becoming indifferent and sometimes isolationist in the face of international responsibilities. Catholic social teaching proclaims that we are our brothers' and sisters' keepers, wherever they live. Learning to practice the virtue of solidarity means learning that "loving our neighbor" has global dimensions in an interdependent world.

A faith community values this when . . .

- it bonds with a sister parish in a Third World country.

- it celebrates Memorial Day and Veterans' Day with the civic community.

- it marks Martin Luther King's birthday.

- it invites missionaries to speak at Sunday Eucharist and supports them financially and with prayer.

Care for God's Creation

The Catholic tradition insists that we show our respect for the Creator by our stewardship of creation. We are called to protect people and the planet, living our faith in relationship with all of God's creation.

A faith community values this when . . .

- it celebrates Earth Day.

- it celebrates Thanksgiving each November and gives thanks for the year's harvest.

- it provides opportunities to collect aluminum cans.

- it encourages parishioners to participate in "spring clean-up days."

- it plants trees on its property and beautifies the parish environment.

Questions to Ponder

While there are times when the faith community needs to come to terms with the challenge of living as disciples, the preacher can also show some new paths that parallel the scriptures of the day. In his book *Imaginal Preaching,* James Wallace offers some excellent avenues for the preacher to approach the texts with fresh eyes and so probe ways that those texts might speak to the needs of the community. On any particular weekend when the preacher feels "stuck," when no message has surfaced over the course of a week's prayer and reflection, these questions are a worthwhile starting point.

How can the images of this text enlighten our lives as a community? What particular darkness do they dispel? How does the image of the text offer prophetic insight?

How does the text offer healing? Does it contain an image that diagnoses our condition or offers hope of cure? What is there in the community that is in need of healing?

Can this imagery take a particular community at this time into contact with "the depths," where it can meet the forces of life and death, of dying and rising? How does this text pull us into a "madness" that can be the source of new creativity for this community? What darkness does it pull us toward? Has it any power to terrorize? Where in this text is the possibility of joy, ecstasy?

How does this text dismember and loosen this community from social constructs that constrain and stifle? What conventions does it overturn? How does it offer liberation and freedom in a way that can overturn and usher in a new kingdom?

How does this text help directly or indirectly to integrate the realm of the repressed? How does it link us with the earth, with the body, with the female and male in all of us, with the soul?

Can this imagery offer the possibility of transformation? From what to what? Does it allow for any epiphany, any sudden revelation? Can this text help to transform social structures in which we have grown comfortable but which are increasingly lifeless, perhaps even death-dealing?

How do the text's images help a community to move onward, to navigate a particular crossroads? What guidance does this image offer?

How does this text through its images convey a message for this community? How is this text a messenger?

How does this text allow the community to engage in play that leads us to ponder the truth of life? What cultural traits can this text address, reinforce, contradict, subvert? How does this text invite us into the analysis of and toying with cultural traits, which has as its goal to draw those present to ponder values, attitudes, behavior? How does this text move the community to think freshly about people, objects, relationships, social roles, the environment?[38]

One of the roles of a spiritual director is to listen and then help the directee to understand how God might be speaking to them in the events of their lives. Having done that, director and directee can then explore together possible paths for the future. As a spiritual director for the faith community, the preacher assumes that same role as the community seeks ways to live in a world of many voices. It is no small gift for a community to have such a person serving it.

 **The Prophet asks, "What significant events have been taking place in the faith community as well as in the local and national communities? What have people been talking about? What light do these scriptures shed upon these events?"**

---

[38] James Wallace, *Imaginal Preaching*, 68–69, 88–89, 111–112. Copyright © 1995, the Redemptorists, published by Paulist Press. Used with permission of Paulist Press.

CHAPTER 9

Presumes That Those Gathered Are Good People

Near the end of *The Fellowship of the Ring,* Frodo stands at the water's edge, having just escaped the pursuing Orcs. He has come to realize that he has been given the ring in order to return it to the fiery place of its forging and so destroy the power of cosmic evil held within it. Yet Frodo is also very much aware of the evil that roams the earth and seeks the ring he carries. He knows well that its maker will stop at nothing to possess it once again. The journey ahead will sap all his strength, and he is afraid. He would gladly turn from the task.

"I wish it need not have happened in my time," he says. "So do I," replies the wizard Gandalf, "and so do all who live to see such times. But that is not for them to decide. All we have to decide is what to do with the time that is given us."[39]

---

[39] J.R.R. Tolkien, *The Fellowship of the Ring* (New York: Houghton Mifflin Harcourt, 2012), 50. Copyright © 1954, 1965 by J.R.R. tolkien. Copyright © renewed 1982 by Christopher R. Tolkien, Michael H.R. Tolkien, John F.R. Tolkien and Priscilla M.A.R. Tolkien. Copyright © renewed 1993 by Christopher R. Tolkien, John F.R. Tolkien and Priscilla M.A.R. Tolkien. Reprinted by permission of Houghton Mifflin harcourt Publishing Company. All rights reserved.

And with that Frodo climbs into the boat and rows to the other side where the journey into the battle with darkness will continue.

Who's in Your Pew?

Most people are good people, at least the ones sitting in the pews are, or they wouldn't be there. Most people want to do the right thing, and when the challenge comes along, as it does for Frodo, they try to rise to the task in spite of the difficulties. This is not to say they are perfect. None of us are. But for the most part we do try. We work at it, and sometimes we succeed with the help of God and sometimes we do not. But we do work at it. Yet preachers can at times be inclined to motivate parishioners to live the gospel out of a sense of guilt.

Consider the fact that among those who sit in the pews every Sunday are a great number of people who struggle to be faithful to the gospel and feel as if they can barely hold on. Why do we seek to add guilt to their already heavy burdens? Among them are:

- the spouse who has been struggling to hold a marriage together for the past five years.

- the man who is just beginning to admit to himself that he may be an addict but is afraid of what life would be like without his addiction.

- the fourth-grader who hates going to school because she is bullied day after day and no one seems to believe her or understand.

- the young man who is engaged to be married in a month but has come to realize that this is not the right person and does not know how to tell anyone.

- the person who hates his job but has a family to support and is too old to be hired by anyone else.

- the elderly person who has been caretaker for a spouse with Alzheimer's for the past five years and is totally worn out.

- the young mother with three preschoolers who cannot stand the tedium and frustrations of raising them and is afraid she might harm them.

- the college student about to graduate who has no idea what he wants to do with his life.

- the high school boy who is gay and can barely admit it to himself much less to anyone else.

- the husband who has lost his job and for the past two months spends the day at the library because he is too ashamed to tell his wife and family.

- the single mom with two children who gets up at five o'clock each morning, takes her children to day care, works all day, comes home to feed them and maintain the home, and at midnight collapses into bed.

- the teenage girl who finds herself pregnant and is being forced by her boyfriend to have an abortion she does not want, but cannot tell her parents.

As preachers we need to find ways to motivate people such as these without adding guilt to the heavy burdens of life they already carry. They come to our churches seeking the strength to live the gospel in the context of the lives with which they are already struggling. They do not need more burdens.

To be sure, not everyone in our faith communities comes with heavy burdens. Many come out of the simple routine of trying to live their lives week in and week out as faith-filled people. Everyone, however, the preacher included, is on a journey in search of life and meaning in that life. Maya Angelou, the contemporary poet who brought her gift of imagery to the first inauguration of President Clinton, made that same observation. "Many things continue to amaze me," she said, "even well into the sixth decade of my life. I'm startled or taken aback when people walk up to me and tell me they are Christians. My first response is the question 'Already?' It seems to me a lifelong endeavor to try to live the life of a Christian. I believe that is also true for the Buddhist, for the Muslim, for the Jainist, for the Jew, and for the Taoist who try to live their beliefs. The idyllic condition cannot be arrived at and held on to eternally."[40]

---

[40] Maya Angelou, *Wouldn't Take Nothing for My Journey Now* (New York: Random House, 1993), 73. Copyright © 1993, Maya Angelou, published by Random House, 1993. Used by permission.

Eucharist means to give thanks. We gather to thank our God for the blessings of life, and I suppose to recognize the blessings we may have missed or passed by. We hope to recognize that we have not been abandoned by God, and to see how God is a part of all that we are about. We want to believe—desperately—that the struggles and difficulties of life are not sent as a punishment for our failures, but rather to see where and how God might be present even amid such struggles and difficulties, and hopefully then to give thanks once we discover that presence.

The Pews in the Vineyard

Often we who preach can presume that those in the assembly are looking for an easy way out. I suppose in one sense we all are; we all try to avoid having to do the difficult thing just because that is what it is—the difficult thing. On the other hand we do want to be good people, and we do work at it. All of us know when we are living the gospel. And all of us know when we should be but are not. None of that means we do not try. Being told one more time will not change us. We are all on a journey, and none of us are at the same place.

All of this is much like the parable of the workers in the vineyard. We are not invited into the kingdom as if it were to some *place*, but rather we are invited into God's presence and into God's way of life. That invitation seems to come at different times of life for different people, and perhaps more than once for all of us. Whenever we say yes, whenever we embrace the life that is offered, then we find the reward of God's love.

"The kingdom of heaven is like a landowner who went out early in the morning to hire laborers for his vineyard. After agreeing with them for the usual daily wage, he sent them into his vineyard. When he went out about nine o'clock, he saw others standing idle in the marketplace; and he said to them, 'You also go into the vineyard, and I will give you what it just.' So they went off. And he went out again around noon and around three o'clock, and did likewise. Going out about five o'clock, he found others standing around, and said to them, 'Why

do you stand here idle all day?' They said to him, 'Because no one has hired us.' He said to them, 'You too go into my vineyard.' When it was evening the owner of the vineyard said to his foreman, 'Summon the laborers and give them their pay, beginning with the last and ending with the first.' When those who had started about five o'clock came, each received the usual daily wage. So when the first came, they thought that they would receive more, but each of them also got the usual wage. And on receiving it, they grumbled against the landowner, saying, 'These last worked only one hour, and you have made them equal to us who bore the day's burden and the heat.' He said to one of them in reply, 'My friend, I am not cheating you. Did you not agree with me for the usual daily wage? Take what is yours and go. What if I wish to give this last one the same as you? Or am I not free to do as I wish with my own money? Are you envious because I am generous?' "
(Matthew 20:1–15)

Everyone finds their way into God's presence at their own pace, or perhaps it is more accurate to say that everyone is invited into God's presence at different times in their lives. So then why criticize God's plans? Why demand that those who seek to live the gospel do it on a timetable that is less than divine?

Some years ago I presided at the wedding of a young couple. They invited me to the reception, and so I happily went. Among the guests at the reception was the groom's great-uncle who was ninety-two years old. Earlier that year the uncle himself had been married—for the first time. He was introduced, and everyone applauded. What a wonderful thing to finally find love. No one complained that he did not find it earlier. No one chided him for waiting so long. Everyone was happy for him. So why is it that we chide others for not yet having found a way to live the gospel the way we think it should be lived? It is God's way of proceeding, not ours. Whenever someone finds such joy in life, we should find ourselves giving thanks with them.

Loving the Folks in the Pews

Perhaps you still think that some people can only be motivated by feelings of guilt, and that there are all sorts of individuals in the pews who need to be guilted into living the gospel. If you think this may be the case, I invite you to try this experiment. Some weekend while you are presiding but not actively engaged at a particular moment, perhaps during some silence or during the singing of a hymn, I invite you to look out over the assembly and identify by name for yourself which specific individuals you think are in need of such motivation. Who do you know in the assembly who is not living out the gospel as best they can? My suspicion is that any of us would be hard put to name someone. The point is that we can never know anyone's story or their life's goodness or lack of it.

The story is told that before a performance the actress Mary Martin would stand backstage peeking out from behind the curtain at the audience as they took their seats, repeating to herself, "I love you. I love you. I love you." She did this, the story goes, because then her performance would take on an entirely different aura as she would more readily put her heart and soul into that evening's production.

Such a practice might be a worthwhile consideration for each of us who preach. If we truly care about those in the pews, if we do love them, if we do realize that they are indeed good people who day by day seek to be better people, how can that not affect our preaching?

 **The Preacher asks, "How does goodness show forth in the lives of these people to whom I preach? Where and when have I seen them trying to live out the Gospel of this Sunday?"**

CHAPTER 10

Leaves the Assembly with Hope

There is something in the human spirit that simply wants to hope. Hoping captures our imaginations, feeds our dreams, and gives us a purpose for living. John Lennon's song "Imagine," with its notion of a world of dreamers joining together in a better future, struck a chord when it was first written. It continues to have a universal appeal, reminding us that we human beings can be more than what we seem to be.

Victor Hugo's *Les Misérables* is in part the story of a failed student uprising in the Paris of 1830 in protest of the reestablishment of the French monarchy. In recent times the novel has become a hugely successful musical and now also a film. In one scene the students gather just before they go out to confront the forces of the establishment. Driven by the dream of a democratic France, they sing of a new day. They hope that the citizens of Paris will be moved to join them in giving birth to democracy. When they do not, the students stand alone, and in the end give their lives to the dream that has overtaken them. They attest to the fact that the world is transformed by people who dream, who live with hope. Conversely, the world is not transformed by people out of a sense of guilt.

It has been the foundation of this book that liturgical preaching is about naming the activity of God in our world, pointing to where God is doing today what God did then in the scriptures we read and hear. As has been noted in *Preaching the Mystery of Faith*, "First, the homilist is speaking to people who are, at least to some degree, searching for Jesus Christ and the meaning that the Gospel can give to their lives. This is what ultimately draws them to the Eucharist, no matter how fragile their faith and understanding might be."[41] When people of faith hear such preaching week after week, they begin to realize that their God is indeed with them, that God is shaping their lives into the image of the Lord Jesus, that they have not been abandoned by God. To know this, then, is to live with hope. To know this is to believe that the future can and will be more than what we see today. To know this is to recognize that all of God's promises have been faithfully kept. "Behold, I am with you always, until the end of the age" (Matthew 28:20).

Preaching to Postmodern Believers

We live in a time of history when hope is hard to come by. Over the course of the last fifty to sixty years the world view of Western culture has undergone a drastic revision. There has been a reversal of modernity, and our culture now exists in what has come to be called the postmodern age. I have found the reflections of Walter Brueggemann extremely helpful in exploring the ways of preaching to a world that has changed so greatly.

We live in a post-literate age, a time when we no longer learn about the world from books. Brueggemann refers to the observations of Stephen Toulmin.[42]

---

[41] *Preaching the Mystery of Faith*, 15.

[42] Walter Brueggemann, *Texts under Negotiation* (Minneapolis, MN: Fortress Press, 1993), 6.

- We have moved from a written culture to an oral culture, from newspapers to television to the internet. Consider the simple fact that 1985 was the last time more books were checked out of libraries than videos were rented, to say nothing of the fact that video rental itself has now become a thing of the past.

- We have experienced a shift from truth as universal to truth as particular, from general to local. "Only my experience matters" has replaced any notion of universal truth.

- There is no grand story that can any longer claim assent. We are left only with local stories.

- All knowledge is pluralistic, with many voices claiming to hold the truth depending upon one's perspective.

Why did this happen? Brueggemann offers four reasons, proposed by Langdon Gilkey, for this shift in world view.

1. Intellectual know-how has failed to deliver the good life.

2. The political promise of the Enlightenment has failed to bring peace and has led to powerful tyranny.

3. The claim of "progress" has not worked out at all convincingly.

4. Confrontation with world religions has shaken the claims and domination of Western religions.[43]

James Zullo has described the consequent world view of the Gen-X generation as having these characteristics:

- There is no such thing as absolute truth.

- There is to life a lack of coherence, and thus many paradoxes.

- There is little faith in institutions. As a result they trust only themselves.

---

[43] Ibid., 6–7.

- Human existence is random, impermanent, nightmarish. Thus they search for meaning and purpose.

- Community has great value.[44]

I do not posit this shift in world view as either good or bad. I am simply pointing out what has taken place and is generally attested to by most observers of culture. This is the world in which we live and the world to which we preach. To ignore this reality is to preach to those in the clouds.

In this environment, doctrinal preaching will hold little attraction for the vast majority of individuals who do not believe in any absolute truth. Appealing to natural law will have little sway among those who do not see any grand story to human life. Attempting to convince by proclaiming the wisdom and authority of the Church and its teachings will not persuade those who are already suspicious of any institutions, including the institution of the Church. How then does the preacher offer hope to those who live with this world view? Again I refer to the work of Walter Brueggemann.

Hoping to Find Hope

Brueggemann argues that

1. People do not change, or change much, because of doctrinal argument or sheer cognitive appeal.

2. People do not change, or change much, because of moral appeal.

3. People in fact change by the offer of new models, images, and pictures of how the pieces of life fit together—models, images, and pictures that characteristically have the particularity of narrative to carry them . . . What is yearned for among us is not new doctrine or new morality but new world, new self, new future.[45]

---

[44] Zullo, James R., "God and Gen-X: Faith and the New Generation." *Seminary Journal* 8, no. 2 (Autumn, 2002): 42–54. Published by the National Catholic Educational Association, 1005 North Glebe Road, Suite 525 Arlington, VA 22201, Telephone: (571) 257-0010, Fax: (703) 243-0025, E-Mail: seminary@ncea.org

[45] Brueggemann, *Texts under Negotiation,* 24–25.

Brueggemann goes on to propose three different ways of imagining ourselves as a means of offering hope to those in the assembly. First, he notes that God has not yet brought us to be all that we can be. We are not finished selves. He proposes that the preacher *"Imagine a self,* no longer the self of consumer advertising, no longer a self caught in endless efforts of self-security, but a self rooted in the inscrutable miracle of God's love, a self no longer consigned to the rat race, but one oriented to full communion with God."

Second, he posits a world that is incomplete, and so then the preacher is to *"Imagine a world,* no longer a closed arena of limited resources and fixed patterns of domination, no longer caught in endless destructive power struggles, but able to recall that lyrical day of creation when the morning stars sang for joy, a world no longer bent on hostility, but under God's presence as a place where creatures 'no longer hurt or destroy.' "

Finally, Brueggemann describes the Church as yet unfinished, and thus the task of the preacher is to *"Imagine a community of faith . . .* drastically renovated" by God's love and presence, both "healed and made safe."[46]

Lest this all be pie in the sky, Brueggemann then adds another dimension. He proposes that preaching articulate God's promise in the face of the world in which we live. In other words, what of God's promise is revealed in the word we hear on this Sunday, and where have we seen that promise being enfleshed? By articulating God's promise, the preacher brings us back to God's word and the vision God has for us and all of creation. By then naming where that vision has begun to take root in concrete reality, the preacher offers hope in the realization that God is continually present and acting among us. By telling the stories of God's activity today, the preacher makes God's presence local and personal. In effect, the preacher is preaching a spirituality for today that enables those in the pews to recognize God's activity in their own world. That reality is not something far off, as if it were a distant daydream, but rather it is already in process, already becoming. What the preacher does is to proclaim both the "kingdom already" and the "kingdom not yet."

---

[46] Ibid., 49–52.

Dancing Out of Darkness

As noted earlier in this chapter, the generations of this age (not unlike generations of every age) are in search of meaning and purpose for their lives. Because the world seems to be changing constantly and as a result truth also seems to be changing constantly, many individuals feel themselves groping through darkness, or at least through shadows that obscure the path they are called to walk.

In 1931, Arthur Schwartz and Howard Dietz teamed up to write a song titled "Dancing in the Dark." The song is not about dancing but about living, about stumbling our way through life as we grope for meaning. The song begins:

Dancing in the dark till the tune ends,
We're dancing in the dark and it soon ends.
We're waltzing in the wonder of why we're here.
Time hurries by, we're here and we're gone,
Looking for the light of a new love
To brighten up the night. I have you, love,
And we can face the music together
Dancing in the dark."[47]

If people were wondering about that in 1931, people are still wondering about that today. The preacher who is both poet and prophet may be one of the few individuals in our society who can offer glimmers of light for their searching. The images offered by the poet can speak to many, each in their own life situations. The vision of the prophet is able to show what so few see—a vision that can light the path we all walk, a path to faith in God. The preacher can be both poet and prophet as well as a source of the hope that so many seek.

---

[47] *Dancing in the Dark* (from "The Band Wagon"), lyrics by Howard Dietz, music by Arthur Schwartz, copyright © 1931 (Renewed), WB Music Corp. and Arthur Schwartz Music Ltd. All rights reserved. Reprinted with permission.

 **The Prophet asks, "What hope do I want to offer the faith community that gathers?"**

A Summary of the Questions

Each chapter concludes with a question from the Poet or the Prophet or the Preacher. As you read through the scriptures of each week and as you bring your own faith to their consideration, the questions themselves can be used in any number of ways—perhaps to give an entrée into their images, perhaps to be a spark for your own prayer, perhaps to be read through in the midst of your homiletic preparation in order to refocus your creativity, perhaps to use as a sort of check list at the end of your preparation.

Where do I find the biblical stories of this Sunday echoed in the personal and communal events of this past week?

Where or how did God's presence surprise me in ways I had not expected or seen before?

How would I describe God's activity in life during the past week?

What aspects of the past week were challenges for me? For parishioners? For the local or national communities? When did we respond with grace?

What one aspect of God's movement in human life as told in this Sunday's scriptures do I want to share with the faithful who gather? If the past week were a novel of God's movement in life, what title would I give it? What will my message be in six words or less?

Out of my prayer with these texts, what has touched my heart and excited me about God's presence? What image or picture describes that excitement?

As a result of my prayer with these scriptures, what wisdom or insight into God's presence have I realized that I was not aware of a week ago?

What significant events have been taking place in the faith community as well as in the local and national communities? What have people been talking about? What light do these scriptures shed upon these events?

How does goodness show forth in the lives of these people to whom I preach? Where and when have I seen them trying to live out the Gospel of this Sunday?

What hope do I want to offer the faith community that gathers?

 May the Lord always be in our ✠ minds and on our ✠ lips and in our ✠ hearts so that we might worthily proclaim the gospel of the Lord Jesus whose disciples we profess to be.

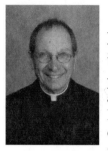 Joseph J. Juknialis is a priest of the Archdiocese of Milwaukee. Throughout his years of ministry he has continued to serve both in parish ministry and in the homiletic programs of Saint Francis de Sales Seminary and the archdiocesan diaconate program. He has written and published a number of collections of stories for use in the classroom and in prayer settings. He provided three years of scripture reflections for *Living the Word*, WLP's annual resource for commentary and meditation on the Sunday and feast day scriptures, and is the author of *Fifteen-Minute Retreats to Slow Down Your World*, published by WLP in 2008. He currently writes a monthly scripture reflection for the Milwaukee archdiocesan newspaper and is a regular presenter at various archdiocesan and parish enrichment and formation programs.